Redikall Crystalline Mind

Inner Resolution for the Outer Revolution

A Guidebook for a Positive Shift in Personal, Spiritual and Professional Life

Strengthen your Foundation for Profound Escalation in Life: A Guidebook

AATMN PARMAR

BALBOA
PRESS
A DIVISION OF HAY HOUSE

Copyright © 2019 Aatmn Parmar

All rights reserved. No part of this book may be used or reproduced by any means, graphic, electronic, or mechanical, including photocopying, recording, taping or by any information storage retrieval system without the written permission of the author except in the case of brief quotations embodied in critical articles and reviews.

The information, ideas, and suggestions in this book are not intended as a substitute for professional advice. Before following any suggestions contained in this book, you should consult your personal physician or mental health professional. Neither the author nor the publisher shall be liable or responsible for any loss or damage allegedly arising as a consequence of your use or application of any information or suggestions in this book.

This book is a work of non-fiction. Unless otherwise noted, the author and the publisher make no explicit guarantees as to the accuracy of the information contained in this book and in some cases, names of people and places have been altered to protect their privacy.

Balboa Press books may be ordered through booksellers or by contacting:

Balboa Press
A Division of Hay House
1663 Liberty Drive
Bloomington, IN 47403
www.balboapress.com
1 (877) 407-4847

Because of the dynamic nature of the Internet, any web addresses or links contained in this book may have changed since publication and may no longer be valid. The views expressed in this work are solely those of the author and do not necessarily reflect the views of the publisher, and the publisher hereby disclaims any responsibility for them.

The author of this book does not dispense medical advice or prescribe the use of any technique as a form of treatment for physical, emotional, or medical problems without the advice of a physician, either directly or indirectly. The intent of the author is only to offer information of a general nature to help you in your quest for emotional and spiritual well-being. In the event you use any of the information in this book for yourself, which is your constitutional right, the author and the publisher assume no responsibility for your actions.

Any people depicted in stock imagery provided by Getty Images are models, and such images are being used for illustrative purposes only.
Fox: Alina Oleynik
Feet image: Olena Pana-sovska
Spine in black: Sahua D
Onions: Arthur Shlain
Pendulum : Carlos Salgado
Ear: Laymik
Rest: Redgreenbee

Print information available on the last page.

ISBN: 978-1-9822-1851-5 (sc)
ISBN: 978-1-9822-1852-2 (hc)
ISBN: 978-1-9822-1853-9 (e)

Library of Congress Control Number: 2018914781

Balboa Press rev. date: 03/22/2019

Dedicated to

All beings who have dedicated their lives to restore love, peace, and harmony on the planet earth

Thrive in Life with a Superconscious Mind

10 Reasons to read this book

Redikall Crystalline Mind (RCM) Book teaches you Redikall Foundation Technique (RFT) to

1. Inspire you to be at your best by motivating your mind to operate at it's best
2. Enhance creativity and clarity in thinking for effective decision-making
3. Enhance stability, harmony and communication in relationships
4. Enable you to live with happiness and joy
5. Improve your focus on your goals and objectives
6. Increase your energy levels to thrive in the material world
7. Propel you to rise and soar high in your consciousness for viewing life objectively
8. Enable you to learn, follow/apply & inculcate sound principles of metaphysics for overall well-being
9. Create space for you to get profound insights and resultant super-refined responses to various challenges
10. Build a strong foundation for heightened evolutionary process, leading you towards personal mastery with Conscious Living

Redikall Crystalline Mind

A powerful bridge between the physical and metaphysical worlds for constant guidance, clarity, peace, and bliss.

People write books for various reasons. Some write to entertain or express beliefs, while others to earn name, fame, and success.

My main intent in writing this book was to create awareness which could manifest a world full of harmony blessed with peace and filled with love and care for self and everyone. When you do not know your precise positioning and direction with respect to others, you are least likely to honor your own unique spaces as well as the unique spaces of others. This often ends up with people rubbing each other the wrong way. The application of **Redikall Reorganization Statements** as a part of overall **Redikall Foundation Technique** explained in this guidebook will certainly assist you in reviving, recognizing, realigning, reorienting, and repositioning yourself so that you can easily raise your awareness and live your life meaningfully, monitored by your superconscious mind in a systematic way.

I was fifteen years old when I started connecting to the metaphysical world. At that time, I had no one to guide me as I tried to analyze the communications I received in different ways. Gradually, as I studied the conscious and subconscious minds through my education as a homeopathic physician from Bombay University and later as a Hypnotherapist from California Hypnosis Institute, all the pieces of the puzzle started falling into place, and I started getting answers to several unanswered questions. Healing myself and others became effortless, and gradually I started withdrawing from the clinical practice as a homeopath and hypnotherapist. I realized that, if people understand the mind correctly and bridge their physical and metaphysical worlds, they will know how to manage themselves and will be empowered to recognize and follow their own guidance and lead meaningful lives. Constant metaphysical guidance and insights are necessary to create a sound foundation for material abundance. The more you wish to rise in life, the more is the need for a deeper and stronger foundation of conceptual clarity and in-depth understanding of mind, metaphysics, and material aspects of human life.

This guidebook is for seekers who wonder *Who am I?* and who attempt to understand their feelings and behavior. It is for those who would like to attract certainty and predictability in their own and others' behavior; who would like to rise beyond all that is happening around them and have an overview of life; for those who are moving on the life path and would like to have assistance from their personalized and intuitive GPS to get the guidance for steering their lives in the right direction. And, finally, it is for those who need a ready guidebook that will help them manage themselves through their routine troubleshooting exercises. Of course, it can also prove to be an invaluable asset for consultants, counselors, and professionals as they work to comprehend and guide their clients in a better way.

This book can assist all who are pursuing spirituality through various disciplines and practices to decode ancient methods in a modern way and progress faster on their chosen path.

Read this guidebook like a recipe book. These are recipes for the mind. No amount of description can give you the necessary experience and taste; you must try them out.

Based on your interest, you can directly refer to any of the following chapters.

Content	Ideal for	Application	Page No.
Part 1: Introduction and Theory	Seekers and researchers who are looking for answers to their intriguing questions related to mind and metaphysics	• Explore answers to the intriguing questions related to mind and metaphysics • Re-read after applying the technique described in Part 2 to reconfirm the theory and apply it in daily life.	1
Part 2: Healing Recipes for Mind Management and personal insights	Self-healing and self-management enthusiasts, healers, Redikall facilitators, mentors, coach, counselors, therapists, professionals, and seekers who would like to avail answers guidance and direction from and through their subconscious mind	• Learn practical application of RFT in personal and professional life • Use as an easy quick reference for professional work, self-healing, and self-management • Apply strategies for effective seeker management	61

Content	Ideal for	Application	Page No.
Appendix I: Keywords of Minor Chakras	Redikall practitioners, Redikall curriculum students, facilitators and mentors	• Use this as a reference once you have grasped and mastered the technique. • For Redikall Practitioners and Facilitators for keyword reference during a session	119
Appendix II: About Redikall© Insights Curriculum	Life-purpose explorers, personal evolution planners	• Learn about planning a journey towards superconscious mind • Learn and grow further through the Redikall Insights curriculum	161
Appendix III: Redikall Reorganization Statements	All	• Logical statements with a magical effect capable of making a profound difference in the state of mind, consciousness, body and outer environment	167
Appendix IV: Redikall FAQs	All	• Answers to Frequently Asked Questions and their answers	169

I express my sincere gratitude to all the team members of Omnipresence Academy of Life Pvt. Ltd.,

For their unconditional support to Redikall Insights.

Wish you a joyous and fulfilling journey inwards to discover the bliss of experiencing your life through the superconscious mind!

Aatmn

The Founder, Director, Omnipresence Academy of Life,

Founder of Redikall © Insights Curriculum

Disclaimer: The copyrighted knowledge in this book is meant to help readers understand erroneous thoughts and emotions behind deviations in the norm. This is not an alternative healing modality; however, this knowledge can complement any other healing modality when used correctly. You are free to use this for yourself and guide others. However, teaching Redikall Foundation Technique without the written permission from the author is strictly prohibited. For details visit: www.redikallhealing.com.

Part 1

Introduction and Theory

CHAPTER 1

About the Guidebook

Have you ever dreamed of a life that

- is free from physical and emotional pain?
- is full of harmony in your relationships?
- is blessed with an easy flow of finances?
- is filled with a deep sense of fulfillment while remaining open to achieve more and succeed on an ongoing basis in all aspects?
- allows you to remain grounded while operating from the higher consciousness?
- inspires you to lead and guide others with clarity?

If you answered yes to many of these points, then this guidebook is just for you. It is a stepping stone to cultivate a super life with a Superconscious Redikall Crystalline Mind.

Aims and Objectives of this Book

- To enable you to grasp and eventually master the Redikall Foundation Technique to lead an overall healthy life.
- To help you revive your true potential with an awareness of your ability to co-create unlimited possibilities.

- To help you recognize, resolve, and refine your response and approach to various inconsistencies in your personal, professional, and social life,
- To help you realign, reorient, and reposition your thoughts to amplify conceptual coherence and optimally use the available resource energies with greater wisdom and total clarity.

You will be empowered to

- understand your mind and mindset, as well as the minds and mindsets of others—and the resultant responses.
- address various health, financial, professional, and relationship challenges with ease and effectiveness.
- practically experience the power of reorganizing your thoughts and resultant beliefs.
- facilitate effective self-management and healing through the Redikall Foundation Technique.
- take a solution-oriented approach to work by arriving at resolutions quickly.
- readily retrieve answers from and through your subconscious mind.
- live with greater insights from your higher consciousness.
- experience an alignment to the collective consciousness.
- lead an overall peaceful, fulfilled, and successful life.

In short, these concepts—and the techniques when successfully applied in your personal as well as professional life—will assist you in navigating your life in an amazingly effective way. You will not only improve your quality of life; you will also motivate others by taking the initiative to make a difference in the world by doing something for the greater good of all.

CHAPTER

2

Introductory Concepts

Every day is a new beginning. Every moment is a new opportunity. It does not matter what your past was like. It is never too late to start something new. It is never too late to do what has not yet been done, to refine what was already fine, and to reorganize all that exists in your life.

Until now, you have been collecting a bunch of experiences, information, emotional impressions, resultant conclusions, beliefs, and preconditionings. Not all of them are of great priority as you shift your perspective, and yet they have formed an important base to bring you where you are today. Let us together address what is yet not addressed. Magnificent creations need clarity of vision and a sound foundation. You are a visionary. You have answers, solutions, and directions to all your queries. At times, they are all hidden like diamonds in the earth's crust.

Let us discover and bring into prominence what is best in you! Let us create a profound base for a prolific life ahead! This foundation is quite sound for you as an individual, a professional, a healer, a metaphysician, or as a keen student of life. We propose to you a way to reorganize your concepts for optimum benefit from all that you have learned so far.

You may have amazing knowledge in the field of healing and mind management; you may have preconceived notions, beliefs, and ways of self-management and therapeutic approaches that have worked for you. However, it would be a good idea to grasp a different perspective rather than looking at the presented knowledge from the perspective of your experiences. Thus, you are requested to remain open to examining a different point of view, experiment on your own, and decide if it suits you in your personal and professional lives. Most precious resources, such as air, water, and sunlight, which are quintessential for life, are easily available in nature; they are very simple to access and easy to use. So is the knowledge of the Redikall Crystalline Mind. Let the ease, simplicity, and applicability prevail in your learning as well as the application of the same.

Self-Management

Are you wondering why suddenly you recognize the need for self-management? Of course, you have been managing yourself quite well in various ways as taught by your parents, society, and an educational system. Why would you find a need to read one more guidebook and look at an additional, different approach? Ask yourself some questions, and you may find a need to learn self-management through the Crystalline Mind: the Redikall Foundation Technique.

- Are you peaceful, relaxed, and composed for the better part of your life?
- Are your relationships working well?
- Are you secure about your finances?
- Are you feeling professionally fulfilled?
- Are you enjoying good health?
- Are you enjoying clarity in your personal and professional lives?
- Are you aware of the purpose of your life? Are you aligned to the purpose of your life?
- Are you happy and joyous most of the time?

If the answer is no to any of these questions, perhaps you need to study this guidebook in depth and apply its teachings until you find that you can answer yes to almost all the questions! It is essential that you integrate your existing self-management efforts with self-healing practices. Effective self-healing is possible when you align yourself radically. That can be achieved by addressing your erroneous thoughts and unhealthy emotional responses—the roots of your issues—where they all begin. To understand your thoughts and emotions, you certainly need to understand the functioning of your mind.

CHAPTER 3

The Crystalline Mind

The prime objective of this guidebook is to assist you with the attainment of the crystalline mindset for living a superconscious life. However, before you understand the process of achieving a crystalline state of mind, it is important to understand the way your mind functions.

Theory of Mind and Metaphysics

This theory is an extension of the "theory of mind" as developed by Dr. John F. Kappas, author of *Professional hypnotism manual: Introducing physical and emotional suggestibility and sexuality.*

Redikall note: The mind is a vastly researched subject. There are several theories developed by various researchers on "mind." Hence, you may find a slight variation in terms of definitions, descriptions, figures, and percentage ratios between the conscious mind and the subconscious mind. In this chapter, you are presented with an adapted model of the theory of mind, with focus on an exclusive practical application for easier comprehensibility not only for Redikall Healing purpose but also for answers to several unanswered questions in life. The clinical application of this model has been repeatedly verified and is presented to you in a simplified manner using the metaphor of computer, internet, and intranet. Appropriate use of this model has the potential to enhance awareness of the physical and metaphysical worlds as well.

The Mind is a Supercomputer

The mind is an abstract energy that can be compared to computer software. Your brain and the nervous system are comparable to hardware, the soul to an operating system, and the higher consciousness to the internet. Just like a supercomputer, all these components work in synergy to effectively manage your thoughts.

The information that follows is the conceptual clarity about the constituents of mind in detail.

All calculations, logical processing, linear thinking, decision making, and resultant actions are processed by your *conscious mind*. Conscious mind is known to be associated with the left hemisphere of the brain. Most individuals operate most of the time out of the conscious mind, which is believed to be a very small fraction of your total mind capacity.

The *subconscious mind* is known to be intricately connected to the right brain, having a creative and artistic approach toward decision making and resultant actions. The subconscious mind is also in charge of ensuring that you remain alive and functional by continuing to evolve in life. Various programs, information, and automated responses to incoming or triggering information are categorically filed in your subconscious mind.

The *filter mind* filters the information flow between your conscious mind and your subconscious mind. The outgoing and incoming information received by all of your senses is filtered by the filter mind based on the rules created based on relevance. For example, sensory inputs from the regular inhalation and exhalation are often deleted or stored in the folder of insignificant information. Any information that is relevant as per the filter mind rules gets directed to an appropriate folder in the subconscious mind. Filter mind operates essentially as a set of rules based on perceptions, judgments, and resultant beliefs that selectively permit the information exchange between your conscious mind and your subconscious mind.

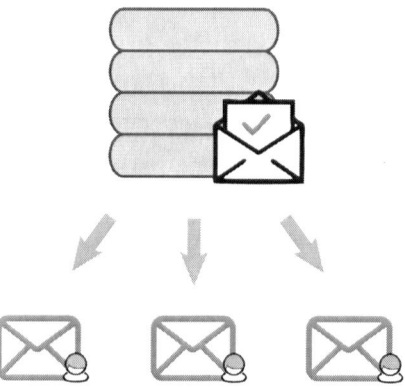

Outgoing information and automated responses are regulated by the filter mind as much as incoming information. These rules can be compared to the rules created in the mailbox of your computer where you decide to store emails in separate folders or send them to the trash, depending on their relevance. When you are relaxed, there is less sensory input so the filtration process is smooth and efficient. When you are emotionally charged, the amount of sensory input increases in an alarming way, which in turn creates a kind of "traffic jam" and chaos in the filter mind. This can also happen when your conscious mind and your filter mind are subjected to sensory information that arrives faster than the usual processing speed; for example, while you are watching a thriller, participating in a concert, commuting on a congested road, or shopping in a supermarket. When your filter mind is partially jammed, the retrieval of information from your subconscious mind may become impossible. For example, you may find it difficult to recall a familiar name when you are stressed with information inflow, or you may inappropriately respond to a friend's remark when you are stuck in a traffic jam. A vicious cycle sets in when your filter mind gets jammed. The retrieval of information and appropriate response system may go unregulated, which in turn creates further complications, increasing the number of sensory inputs, adversely affecting the filtration, like a spillover mechanism. Some information can bypass your filter mind, causing inappropriate storage and random retrieval of information from your subconscious mind. On the contrary, when you are totally relaxed and comfortable, you can retrieve stored information selectively, easily, and appropriately. In a relaxed state of mind, when your filter mind is comparatively clear, you can have better access to the guidance, solutions, and directions from your subconscious mind or through your subconscious mind for an appropriate response to challenging situations in life. Hence, in a relaxed space, your responses to external stimuli are meaningful and constructive in nature. When you meditate or relax, you provide the opportunity for the filter mind to decongest. At the same time, your decongested filter mind often lets you experience a deep state of relaxation.

The tendency to be stressed is directly proportional to the complexity of your filter mind, based on the nature as well as the number of rules, which in turn are determined by beliefs and conditionings that regulate the filtration process. People with fewer beliefs, conditionings, rules, and expectations are more relaxed, clearer in their insights, and more predictable in their approach. However, a certain level of regulation through your filter mind is required to regulate the inflow and outflow of information and responses on an ongoing basis. Optimum rules are also needed for smooth functioning of your filter mind. Your filter mind often becomes more stringent and rigid with aging; hence, as we grow older, the speed of learning reduces and may adversely be affected by several preconditionings.

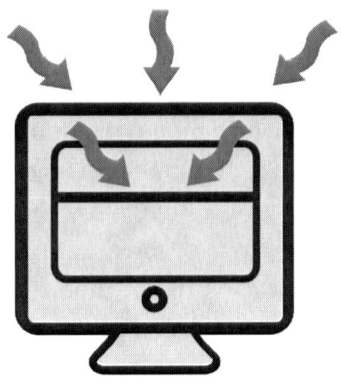

A lot of information is rejected by the filter mind of an adult due to a strong set of conditionings based on past experiences and resultant beliefs. With aging, a strong sense of right and wrong, useful and useless, meaningful and meaningless, good and bad develops. Since infants and children have filter minds that are in the developmental stage, they receive all information without judgment; they can store this information without prior preconditionings. Adults need to be careful in their communication and behavior in the presence of growing children, as the judgments, beliefs, and adverse statements made by them could directly be imprinted in young subconscious minds due to insufficiently developed filter mind. Comments, labels, responses, judgements, education, parenting styles, and training given to young ones by adults—parent figures, influencing personalities, and teachers—greatly influence the formation of their filter minds. After basic formation of the filter mind in nascent stages, very little is contributed towards further development of prime rule formation, as the reformatting of the filter mind could be a challenging task in adulthood. Prime rule formation, or core rule formation, eventually determines the allowance as well as the rejection of information exchange between the conscious mind and the subconscious mind. While the core filtration rule may not easily change in an adult, you can definitely attempt to keep the filter mind clear and decongested to ensure appropriate storage, easy recall, and greater clarity. Yoga, meditation, healing, breathwork, and similar practices help in decongesting the filter mind to a great extent. It has been clinically observed that the Redikall Foundation Technique can influence and restructure the filter mind if used in an appropriate manner.

The Redikall Insights Curriculum is designed to:

- Refine the functioning of the filter mind
- Suitably modify some of the rules to facilitate an easy access and the assistance from the metaphysical world with higher awareness and enhanced consciousness through the subconscious mind
- Equip you with self-management techniques to evolve further and eventually lead a superconscious life

The Subconscious Mind and its Storage System

Information is systematically stored and filed in the subconscious mind using a discreet storage system which can be compared to a master folder. You store experiences in different subfolders according to the information received, filtered and categorized for the purpose of storage in corresponding folders such as good experiences, bad experiences, friendly people, hostile people, safe stuff, and unsafe stuff. The response rules are determined and automated for every folder and storage unit. For example, if information of a particular place is filed in a folder labeled "Unsafe", you automatically remain on guard when you reach that particular place. If a deity is filed in a folder labeled "Protector", you feel safe when you think of that deity, and your responses shift accordingly.

People, places, and possibilities are not your real problems, but the filing system—the resultant associations and the consequent responses to them—are. If the storage system is deranged, the corresponding responses are likely to be dysfunctional and irrational. Your associations, based on the storage system, determine your emotional and behavioral responses. For example, if a person called John has publicly insulted you and humiliated you in the past, you associate John with insults and humiliation because of where you store his memory in your storage mechanism. You are likely to feel upset when you interact with anyone whose name is John or who resembles John. If John is from a particular nation or a town, you may avoid all people belonging to that nation or town. It is possible to respond more appropriately by dissociating John from all adverse associations. The reorganization of the storage system is highly essential for a refined response system. The subconscious mind is preprogrammed to react based on a certain folder-specific trigger. Any element or impression stored in the "Dangerous" folder can initiate a defensive response trigger; for example, a snake, fire, or height. You will learn to refine the response by reorganizing the subconscious mind filing system in the current course of Redikall Crystalline Mind by mastering the art of application of the Redikall Foundation Technique as discussed later in this guidebook. Once the storage system is organized, you can easily download compatible and useful information as well as programs for further benefit.

Redikall note: In the Essential Redikall Insights Course, you will learn the skills and techniques you will need to download compatible programs. (Appendix II)

The Archive Mind

The archive mind is a collection of dormant memories and select preprogrammings. You do not access this part of the subconscious mind frequently. It stores some of the memories related to extremely painful and traumatic experiences. It also archives some of the past-life preprogrammings, which may remain dormant until you have experienced a triggering event. The trigger throws open some of the hidden files and preprogrammings thereby initiating—at times—an irrational response system. Phobic reactions are often due to past-life preprogrammings stored in the archive mind. Many of us are born with some of these preprogrammings. These are inherited based on the experiences of ancestors as well as reference material from the universal library. These are compiled from the experiences of people who lived in the past and have added to the collection of experiences, observations, beliefs, judgments, incompletions, guilts, regrets, fears, and prejudices of all people who have lived in the past. This may be known as collective unconscious or past-life preprogramming. At times, during spontaneous regression or while therapeutically regressing a subject, we can access the information from the experiences of people who died years back with incompletions, guilt, or regrets. Although this information is often believed to be past-life memories, it is difficult to prove. What is revealed as a possible past life may not be the past life of the same individual who was clinically regressed or who has spontaneously regressed. It would be ideal to treat this information, which seems like past-life cellular memories stored in the archive mind, as a metaphor for further therapeutic work instead of being subjective about the stories unfolding through seeming past-life visions. We have found that these preprogrammings are strategically borrowed or downloaded from the universal library or a pool of information to create a profound "project" called life experiences. For example, a person who has a tendency to feel helpless may borrow an experience of a past-life personality who felt helpless or suffered from the guilt of making others feel helpless. In another example, a person seeking to be a leader might borrow a past-life preprogramming of a leader. The discussion of preprograming and past-life regression is out of the purview of this guidebook and shall be discussed in depth in the Advanced Redikall Consciousness course. Right now, it is important to know that the archived memories often get triggered. These programs are not to be tampered with or deleted without recognizing and applying the associated brilliance in them. However, we need to diligently deploy these preprogrammings with higher awareness to take advantage of the optimum benefits from them.

The Soul

The soul can be compared to the operating system. The soul is that program or energy that keeps the brain, body, and mind functional and in sync to ensure that you serve the purpose of your creation. Soul is an extension of the higher consciousness or a larger system in connection to the prime resource energy, which we may understand collectively as God or a metaphor for cloud consciousness.

The Cloud Consciousness

All souls and minds are eventually connected to the cloud consciousness, which can be thought of as the internet connection. You have access to a pool of information through this connectivity. At will, you can download important programs, upgrade your existing system, and run a scan that checks for and eliminates incompatible downloaded programs or information. You merely must establish an aware and conscious connection to this pool. Congestion in the filter mind, over-storage, or an erratic storage system often slows down your connectivity to cloud consciousness and hampers your access to the precious information, timely assistance, periodic upgradation, and corrective measures required in day-to-day life.

Intranet Connection

You are constantly in touch with others' thoughts, beliefs, and ideas through your unaware connectivity at the subconscious or unconscious level. Your mind is intricately connected to the minds of other individuals in your space; therefore, when they shift, your thinking and response towards them shift as well. For example, your unhealthy thoughts about a person in your space will invite a corresponding response from him or her. As you shift your thought, you are likely to manifest changed responses. The reverse is also possible. This explains your distinctive behavioral responses towards various people in the same context. This is further elaborated in Redikall postulates.

States of Mind

Mind can be classified as dysfunctional, functional, and superconscious depending on its ability to respond to situations and experiences. These states are not constant or totally compartmentalized. However, with practice, you can strive to attain and retain a state of functional mind and ultimately a superconscious mind. The beginning can happen as you start working with Redikall reorganization statements as described in Appendix III of this guidebook.

Dysfunctional mind: Under certain circumstances and due to various reasons, the mind may become dysfunctional. The following attributes are observed most commonly in the dysfunctional mind.

- Lack of conscious discretion in the inflow and outflow of information

- Rigid or incorrectly programmed filter mind causing deranged or retarded filtration of information between the conscious and subconscious minds
- Inappropriate filing system generating irrational reactions or set of responses
- Unaware and unregulated access to the archive mind
- Incompatible download of programs and information interfering with the operating system
- Lack of conscious connectivity to the cloud consciousness
- Accessing unhealthy information, which could initiate a system breakdown
- Unmonitored information exchange and interference through the intranet

Functional mind: The functional mind serves the purpose and remains functional in the most appropriate ways under various circumstances. The functional mind is observed to easily do the following:

- Collect all the relevant information well
- Filter the information appropriately
- Store information systematically for easy reference and retrieval
- Look after the constant growth, safety, and well being
- Respond rather than react
- Serve the purpose of life effectively

Superconscious mind: The superconscious mind is an aware mind. The superconscious mind does the following:

- Is aware of all the preprogramming as well as its application and functionality
- Has conscious access to the dormant mind or pool of information from the cloud consciousness
- Selectively accesses and downloads information according to individual compatibility
- Remains a detached observer as well as conscious responder

- Can pre-empt the possibilities and proactively respond with intuitive wisdom
- Is aware of the higher purpose and the roleplay of an individual in the given situation
- Remains totally aligned to serve as per the purpose of life

Presently, you are operating from either a dysfunctional mind or a functional mind. The objective of this guidebook is to inspire you to evolve from a dysfunctional mind to a functional mind and eventually operate as a personality with the Superconscious Redikall Crystalline mindset as explained in following pages.

Different Mindsets

Your mindsets are response patterns to the composite influence of several factors in your life since birth. These include influences from social, economic, cultural, and educational systems. Let us examine the characteristics of a crystalline—(diamond)—mindset vs. the characteristics of a charcoal mindset. Though there is an appropriateness of all that is, in a large scheme of evolutionary pattern, if you still choose to refine your current mindset into a crystalline mindset, the Redikall Insights Curriculum, using various techniques, can systematically guide you to develop the same.

Charcoal and diamond share the same base element, and that is carbon. The difference between diamond and the charcoal is the arrangement and placement of the molecules of the essential element carbon. A scattered arrangement of the molecules in charcoal tends to absorb light and remain amorphous. Organized molecules of diamond radiate light, making it radiant, compact and tough and crystalline in appearance. Though charcoal cannot be readily converted into a diamond, the mind can certainly be transformed from a charcoal mindset to a crystalline diamond-like mindset.

Characteristics of charcoal mindsets and crystalline (diamond) mindsets:

Charcoal Mindset	Crystalline (Diamond) Mindset
Susceptible to repeated breakdowns or a burnt-out feeling due to overuse due to its fragility	Strong and powerful
Succumbs to external adversities and impacts	Endures the effects of environmental adversities and impacts
Remains vulnerable to detrimental factors	Remains vulnerable to people with Crystalline mindsets
Creates a superficial impression on others	Impressive with an ability to sharply negotiate with others
Often feels taken for granted, unimportant, undervalued, and exploited by others	Valued, cherished, and treasured by others
Non-transparent, foggy, clogged—unable to reflect light	Transparent— reflects, radiates and amplifies light (light is a metaphor for knowledge and awareness)
Rigid, unrefined, and disorganized filter mind	Flexible, refined, and organized filter mind
Preprogrammed archive mind	Minimal or no archive mind
Incoherence; lack of sync between the conscious mind, filter mind, subconscious mind, and the operating system	Coherent; cooperation and super connectivity between the conscious mind, subconscious mind, filter mind, and the operating system
Absorbs as well as retains all the information and emotional impressions	Selective information processing, transmission and storage; appropriate emotional impressions

Charcoal Mindset	Crystalline (Diamond) Mindset
Dull, lack of clarity, and often confused, lacking focus, diffused	Sharp, great clarity and highly focused
Prejudiced, judgemental, narrow-minded, opinionated with a tendency to be indifferent	Unbiased, non-judgemental, open-minded, distant observer with active participation
Highly prone to easy exhaustion resulting in fatigue	Agile, active, and resilient

Charcoal and diamond share the same base element, and that is Carbon.

The difference between the diamond and the charcoal is …

The arrangement and placement of the molecules of the essential element 'Carbon'.

A scattered arrangement of the molecules in charcoal tends to absorb light and remain amorphous.

Organized molecules of diamond radiate light, makes it radiant, compact and tough.

Though, as of now, a charcoal cannot be converted into a diamond, the mind can certainly be transformed from a Charcoal mindset to Crystalline/Diamond Mindset.

Are You Ready for the Transformation?

As I have mentioned, practically it is not possible to convert a piece of charcoal into a diamond, but you can certainly convert a charcoal mindset into a diamond-like crystalline mindset with ease and awareness. Please refer to the characteristics of these mindsets, outlined in the table above, to help you understand the best possible transformation using the Redikall Foundation Technique.

Yes, the transition from a charcoal mindset to a crystalline (diamond) mindset takes quite a bit of diligent self-management work; however, you can begin by thoroughly understanding the sound principles of mind management and metaphysics.

CHAPTER 4

Metaphysics

Whatever is beyond physics is known as metaphysics. Your mind is essentially trained to operate in a finite manner based on all your sensory inputs. These inputs can be validated by others and proved by existing scientific parameters as well. Though you predominantly use your conscious mind in your day-to-day functioning, the versatility of conscious mind is quite limited. Your subconscious mind has a greater potential but still remains unavailable to the conscious mind for routine functioning. As you transcend your consciousness, you explore a vast realm of metaphysical frequencies which do not have any physical existence and can be neither conceived by your senses nor proved by science as of now. There were several scientific theories and discoveries which, in the past, were rejected by science until they were proven to be true. Examples are gravity, the moon being a satellite, and the Earth being round. You can wait until science validates metaphysical findings or you can, in the meantime, discover practical applications that can enhance and enrich the experience of life in the most beneficial and practical manner.

Who Explores the Metaphysical Realm?

People have their own reasons for exploring and accessing the metaphysical world. A lot depends upon their preprogramming, past incompletions, and at times, mere curiosity to discover or disprove the occult. Some may have a need to search for the meaning of life, whereas others maybe exploring metaphysics to escape their current physical reality.

- **Curiosity:** A desire to know about "life beyond life" may lead to the exploration of metaphysics. People under the effect of narcotics or similar substances tend to bypass the filtration process of the filter mind. They attempt to connect with the higher altered frequencies or consciousness to seek experiences which are beyond their limited perceptions and the boundaries of the physical realm.
- **Unanswered questions:** An inability to get satisfactory answers and explanation through their logical minds in the paradigm of the physical realm often leads people to explore the metaphysical realm. Questions such as these may inspire exploration: What's the purpose of my life? Why am I getting attracted to someone? Why do I feel or experience differently than others? Why do good people suffer or die so early?
- **A desire to connect to the departed ones:** At times, people desire to connect to people who have left their bodies, yet their presence is perceived by some in their earthly space. This perception may inspire exploration into the unexplored realms.
- **Spiritual quest:** The metaphysical world is often explored as a means of personal and spiritual growth. Most meditators connect to the metaphysical zone in their meditative space. Some meditators and spiritual seekers explore this realm often to connect to the frequencies in pursuit of unanswered questions and to avail themselves of guidance from higher intelligence and for increasing their awareness via consciousness expansion. Psychics often explore the metaphysical world for the purpose of getting information which the filter mind of those who are not psychic may not permit because of preset rules. Some psychics who are not spiritually evolved may retrieve and share information to match their mindsets or suit their beliefs and may fail to see the brilliance in the larger plan. Because of this, they may misguide seekers by accessing and sharing contaminated knowledge. It is important to note that not all who call themselves psychics are spiritually evolved, and not all spiritually evolved people have psychic abilities.
- **Therapeutic benefits:** Exploration of past lives, parallel realities, and foreign energy management for the therapeutic purpose may

be the first introduction to the metaphysical world for many individuals.
- **The desire for powers:** Some people, based on the belief that one can be more powerful by conquering or communicating to the unknown, discover ways and means to explore the metaphysical world.
- **Companionship:** Loneliness may compel some to befriend metaphysical elements. They may begin as fantasy figures who fill the void for companionship. Soon there may be an increased need to explore further in the unseen universe.
- **Escapism:** When the outer world becomes boring, painful, unbearable, shameful, and unpleasant in general, people may have a tendency to escape into the metaphysical realm. Schizophrenics, people addicted to psychotropic drugs, people suffering from clinical psychosis or paranoid personality disorders could all belong to this category. In some of these cases, people lose the distinction between the physical world and the metaphysical world and this can create an imbalance in the present reality.

Why Should You Explore the Metaphysical World?

As GPS has made your travel easier, in the present context, being well connected to the metaphysical realm could make your journey through what we call life quite easy and effortless. When you follow the higher guidance, you seldom invite friction, collision, or trouble. You can anticipate the adversities well in advance and are often directed to safe detours when they are required during your journey. For example, metaphysically connected people have total cognizance of their bodily needs for nourishment and rest. They can anticipate needs in advance and nurture their bodies accordingly. The same is true with their relationships or finances. With higher consciousness, they have the ability to anticipate the possibility of upcoming conflicts or difficult times and steer away smoothly during the turbulent phases in their relationships or professional lives. Your life can be fairly smooth, easy, and joyous as you continue to be guided through various experiences in a meaningful way. You also need to periodically cleanse, keep abreast with the latest upgrades, and remain connected to the remote frequencies for an exchange of vital information in a safe and secure way. All this can happen spontaneously through various spiritual practices or through healing. Healing through Redikall Insights helps you clear the blockages and barriers to unite you with your highest consciousness; hence, Redikall way of healing could be a form of yoga. *Yoga* means "union"—your union with your higher consciousness. Redikall Insights help you heal in a radical manner by healing and integrating all that is unhealed in your space. (Appendix IV)

A Word of Caution for Metaphysical Explorers!

Exploration of the metaphysical world can be compared to the exploration of a jungle without a guide, map or GPS. You are likely to stray! This aimless and unescorted search can also be compared to internet exploration without any plan or objective. You not only stumble upon interesting information; at times, you come across destabilizing information. However, if exploration is deployed judiciously, it can enlighten you and provide helpful information from the highest consciousness. Most drug addicts and narcotic substance abusers, in a hurry to explore the metaphysical world, use a shortcut under the influence of their drug of choice because some of these chemicals bypass the filter mind rules. Spiritual seekers achieve the same in a systematic manner by safely reorganizing the filter mind. The kind of elemental frequencies you tune in to depends upon your intent of alignment to them through a subtle antenna, which generates a particular experience or aligns with a set of information. When you explore through artificial means such as narcotic substance, go unescorted or without proper guidance, you may wander aimlessly and find it difficult to adjust back to the physical world. The intent behind the metaphysical exploration is vitally important to achieve the desired end results.

Spirituality is not an aimless escape in the metaphysical realm. Spirituality is a systematic study of the ultimate spirit (energy) – The prime resource energy.

What you explore in the metaphysical world is highly influenced by your emotional needs, your beliefs, your preprogrammings, your objectives, and finally, a level of healing and personal evolution. If you explore while you are incomplete, scattered, and unhealed, you are likely to access information which will scatter you even more and may leave you feeling more unhealed. If you explore metaphysics to avoid emotional upheavals, you are likely to multiply them eventually. When you explore this world as "whole" and "complete", you are likely to get in touch with the frequencies that will enhance and reinforce the experience of being whole and complete. Even though it may require a certain level of patience to heal yourself sufficiently to feel whole and complete, it is worth all the effort and perseverance because the awareness and the conscious knowledge will be available to you in the highest and purest form. If a part of you is unhealed—has a belief, judgment, or emotional charge—the incoming pure information and insights could either become filtered or contaminated so they may not be of the purest nature.

Most people are driven to explore the metaphysical world at times when they are disturbed, disillusioned, or disgusted with the physical world. Some people explore this world after completing all their needs for physical level experiences. The level of saturation leads to boredom and inspires them to explore and learn about the unknown. Some people do not find the need to go beyond the material realm; consequently, they spend their entire lives totally immersed in material experiences. Their minds are like those computers that are meant for specific functions such as accounts, architectural designs, or games. Though these computers may never connect to the internet, they can still function well and serve the purpose of their existence. Some people accidentally or randomly connect to the metaphysical world just like a radio, that tunes in to an unknown frequency. They become channels of information for those who are yet to connect to those frequencies. In these cases, the information is often incoherent or contaminated by the values, judgments, and rules set by their filter minds. Eventually, they let the flow of resourceful information and frequencies flush out or transform the contamination till the time they eventually emerge as channels of pure awareness, remaining connected to the highest level of consciousness.

Redikall Perspective of Past Lives

Past lives may be described as the experiences, incompletions, observations, beliefs, and conditionings borrowed from individuals who have lived their lives in the past. A lot of research and therapeutic work has been done by various people with respect to past lives. Some cultures and religions endorse the existence of multiple lives while some do not. After the death of an individual, as the physical body merges with physical elements, the thoughts, beliefs, observations, and experiences are compiled and added to the collective pool of information available in the universal libraries for download and reference. There are reasons for an individual to connect to certain types of "preprogrammed past lives" during certain phases of life. However, we propose to view past life as a preprogramming necessary for those experiences necessary for your current life purpose and existence. For example, an individual with a need to take a leadership role in the current life may borrow the preprogramming of an individual who has been a successful leader in the past. However, if the past life character has died due to a political conspiracy, the preprogrammed individual may have the potential to be a leader and, at the same time, may experience inhibition because of subconscious fear of taking up a leadership role. Clinically, we can regress the person and dissociate death with leadership by the technique taught in the Advanced Redikall Consciousness Curriculum. Meanwhile, with <u>Redikall Reorganization</u> statements, you can easily address them as described in Part 2 of this guidebook.

Redikall note: More information on past life and regression work is available in the Advanced Redikall Consciousness Course (www.redikallhealing.com).

Redikall Perspective on Parallel Realities and Parallel Life

Parallel reality—or parallel life—is an experience derived from our own experiences or those of other people who exist parallel to us in different parts of the world or realms. You can subconsciously and metaphysically connect to these entities in order to go through the experiences that you have been fantasizing about or to satisfy the need to complete certain incomplete learnings at the soul level. We may zone into another individual's life as a computer would connect to another computer through the intranet. Ups and downs experienced by a personality in a parallel life may interfere with, add to, or complicate the experiences of an individual who is connected to that parallel life. Many a time, personal incompletion and curiosity may metaphysically connect you to another person's life. For example, a person with an incomplete desire to be a successful athlete may be led to metaphysically connect to the experiences generated by a successful athlete. Phenomena like these could be the reason behind a periodic feeling of disappointment or joy of victory without corresponding circumstantial evidence or experiences in the current reality. An experienced Redikall facilitator can seek the brilliance behind the need for the parallel life and align to that instead of disconnecting or rejecting the parallel life.

Parallel life can be compared to a master computer with various windows open on different display screens that are a metaphor for different worlds or realms. To expand the metaphor, we can say that, at times, when there is an urgent need to add a certain programming functionality, instead of installing a program, you may get connected through an intranet or the internet. The parallel life connectivity helps in sharing certain information, programs, and functions for the desired output without any need for upgrades or program downloads.

Redikall Perspective of Negativities and Their Influence

What appears to be negative to some people may be positive to others, and what appears to be positive to some may be negative for others. Hence, negativity and positivity are subjective perceptions. For example, carbon dioxide, which is often perceived as harmful or negative, is necessary for stimulating the inhalation also for the survival of plants. It is reprocessed into oxygen, which is, in turn, consumed as the next breath by all living beings. Essentially, any experience that inspires you to live life fully is perceived as positive in nature. If you are experiencing negativity from family members, friends, other people, the environment, or the workplace around you, you should reconsider your perspective as you may not be able to change the people or circumstances directly. However, you can certainly address your sensitivity, perception, and resultant response towards them. As you start addressing your needs using the Redikall Foundation Technique, you will find a positive shift in your thinking and resultant responses, which in turn brings about a positive shift in your environment. This will eventually bring about a modification in the experiences related to associated people and events.

Redikall note: In the Essential Redikall Insights Course (www.redikallhealing.com), you learn to identify negative thoughts and appropriately modify your own anchoring thoughts, which manifest the negativity in your external and inner space.

Redikall Perspective on Foreign Energies, Ghosts, and Spirits

Foreign energies, ghosts, and spirits—these terms are interchangeably used to define the existence of what I call "thought forms with emotional charge related to incomplete desire, guilt and regret" experienced by certain sensitive and vulnerable ones. Inadequate scientific evidence of their presence has made them highly controversial, yet the fact remains that many people sense them around. Some people are able to establish a connection with them on a regular basis. Some people believe they are merely fictional and creation of individual imaginations. When the soul leaves the body, the deceased ones' powerful thoughts, emotions, and beliefs may float around in the physical space. Many people feel scared and troubled and try to push these entities away perceiving them to cause harm according to previously learned beliefs. It is best to treat these entities like bundles of thoughts or emotions without a physical body. Their existence beyond their bodies can be explained as software without hardware, and your software can connect to them just as it can connect to any other internet program. The experience you generate due to this connectivity is quite in sync with your life experience in general. For example, if you have a tendency to feel helpless or insecure, these entities could make you feel helpless or insecure as well. In short, they give you an experience similar to the one you would eventually experience or may even be experiencing already. Hence, they are your projection and extension due to your need for the experience. Even if you harbor disbelief related to their existence, it is important to address the adverse nature of perception, experience, and resultant response generated towards them. They, directly, may not be your issue, but your need to feel helpless or insecure would certainly be your issue. If you are feeling intruded upon by them, perhaps you could be feeling intruded upon by many other (living) people around you. Address your need for feelings such as helplessness, insecurity, or exploitation, and these thought forms may not trouble you as they might be just your projection and supporting your need for certain experiences. As and when you rise beyond, your need for certain experiences, you may not perceive them in your space. One metaphor for these thought forms is germs floating in the air. Even if they are all around you in your space, they will affect you adversely only according to your vulnerability to them. These can also be perceived as energy frequencies and thought forms. Not all of them are harmful and adverse in nature. In fact, some of them are quite helpful and are meant to assist you in maintaining equilibrium. Some of the guiding and helpful energies are popularly known as angels and ascended masters.

Redikall Perspective on Black Magic, Evil Eye, and Voodoo Spells

Black magic, evil eye, and voodoo spells are likely to be the culmination of very powerful thought energies with the desire for destructive end results. First of all, providing evidence or proof of their existence may be difficult. In most of the cases that have been addressed by Redikall Insights, it was found that black magic, at times, can be an end result of the paranoid ideas that people have for several subjective reasons. Some of the reasons are ancestral and cultural beliefs, guilt of doing better than others, past experiences of being targeted for being an outstanding performer, or guilt from having harmed others in the past in a similar way. Even if they are paranoid in nature, even if they are mere perceptions and not reality, even if they are so-called fictional or fragmented reality, considering that the outer world is our extension, working on black magic and people who are doing black magic can be meaningless. As soon as you address one instance, another one could crop up soon. They are possibly responding to your need for perception, experience as well as validation of pre-existing or pre-programmed beliefs.

You can recognize your precise causative and anchoring thoughts through the Essential Redikall Insights Course and address them radically. You can also discover the purpose and brilliance of their perception, creation, and existence in the Advanced Redikall Consciousness Course. Meanwhile, you can heal your perception and response patterns with the help of the Redikall FoundationTechnique(www.redikallhealing.com).

CHAPTER 5

What is Healing?

To heal literally means to become whole and complete.

Healing is an experience of becoming whole, complete, and in harmony with the inner as well as the outer world. Healing is not necessarily "fixing", but when you feel whole, complete, and in harmony, you become aligned to that which is whole, complete, and in harmony—the prime resource energy—in an effortless and natural restorative manner. For years, *healing* has been a synonym for fixing, curing, and alleviating illness. Hence, most individuals have never found a need to heal themselves on a regular basis; rather, they have waited until their health, finances, or relationships have suffered.

> ***As you cleanse and nurture your body daily, you need to cleanse, organize, and nurture your mind regularly too.***
>
> ***Periodically keep connecting to the cloud consciousness for constant upgradation and restoration.***
>
> ***Effortlessly remain synchronized with other operating systems through your connectivity with the universal operating system.***

To summarize, healing is an experience of feeling whole and complete by becoming aligned to that which is whole and complete, which is the universal operating system—the ultimate pool of consciousness—so that we remain functional by reviving, recognizing, realigning, reorienting, and repositioning ourselves as per the co-designed role play to restore the harmony in our inner and outer space.

The Healing Experience

Any experience that makes you feel whole and complete is healing in nature. During pregnancy and after birth, several times due to exposure to traumas of various kinds, the experience of being whole and complete becomes adversely affected. These traumas could be in the form of physical injury, emotional hurt, social isolation, financial devastation, political challenges, legal hurdles, or spiritual misalignment. Most of the time, you tend to live your entire life with the post-traumatic effect. Fortunately, the benevolent universal resource energy heals all. However, there are times when you consciously or subconsciously remain unavailable to the healing energy and go through various types of discomfort in different aspects of life.

> *20 percent of your problems and challenges in life are brilliantly pre-designed to be stepping stones instead of roadblocks.*
>
> *The remaining 80 percent of the issues are due to your ignorant reactions caused by the rejection of problems and challenges.*
>
> *Enhanced awareness enables you to perceive your problems and challenges as opportunities to make positive shifts in life.*
>
> *Most of the events and experiences that you perceive as adverse have been carefully predesigned in your life and are meant to be stepping stones rather than roadblocks.*

Your adverse response system is based on a previously learnt and experienced set of misconceptions as well as ignorance and unawareness filed in the storage system of your subconscious mind. This response system, when triggered, eventually results in different sorts of emotional disturbances at the conscious-mind level. The energy of these disturbed emotions, along with information overload from body sensations created by overtly disturbed emotions, eventually blocks the filter mind. This is when you lose the conscious connectivity with the subconscious mind, metaphysical realm, and higher consciousness, resulting in obliteration of the visionary clarity from your higher consciousness to perceive several events and experiences in life in a better light. There is a reason and a brilliance embedded in all that happens to you. Only when you clear the filter mind, retrieve and sort out the dormant information from your archive mind, and review the past from your higher consciousness point of view, you can beautifully have glimpses of the magnificence in the so called "maddening" experiences of the past or present.

Here is an opportunity to:

- Revive the benumbed and suppressed parts of your personality.
- Recognize those parts that need healing.
- Realign yourself to the flow of powerful healing of the prime resource energy.
- Reorient yourself towards higher thinking and healthy living.
- Reposition yourself to be constantly in sync with the prime resource energy.

In order to undertake healing, one does not have to be ill or uncomfortable.

> *Healing is for all.*
> *Healing is a soul-and-mind-bathing experience.*
> *Even if you are healthy, you need regular healing*
> *as much as you need regular bathing.*
> *You certainly deserve it! You owe it to yourself!*

To summarize, your soul and mind need to be aligned with the flow of healing energy as frequently and regularly as your body requires bathing and cleansing.

Redikall Postulates

These postulates are conclusions that were established after repeated observations and clinical verifications of cases resolved by trained experts using various Redikall techniques. They may be similar in terms of observation, description, and conclusion to thoughts of other authors and researchers also. Without claiming to be the prime authority, it is best to introduce you to these postulates with reference to the Redikall philosophy and clinical observations.

- All that exists has an appropriate space and role to play in our lives. Whether we like it or not, with our limited logical thinking, what exists has been sanctioned at some level of existence by us. We have created a space for it.
- There is no good or bad. If things are not working well for you, you need to revive, recognize, realign, reorient, and reposition them. Alternatively, you can revive, recognize, realign, reorient, and reposition yourself or your responses. A crude example is a need for a waste paper basket. If you keep it in the middle of your bed it could be a nuisance, but if you place in a more convenient position with the right orientation and alignment, it can be of value for collecting your trash.
- There is a harmonious flow within a brilliantly designed system which is beneficial for all, provided people do not interfere with their human idiosyncrasies caused by insufficient awareness of the larger plan.
- To bring about a shift in the external universe, you must initiate a shift within. As you shift, the external environment shifts.
- What you resist tends to persist; what you recognize tends to get reorganized. Your problems may continue to persist when you resist. When you drop the resistance and give due recognition to your problems, the situation changes, modifies, and alters to match your needs, expectations, and requirements. You can validate this for yourself when you practically apply these postulates in your daily life and Redikall Facilitation.
- It is impossible to destroy anything, but it is possible to transform anything. This postulate is based on Einstein's theory of the interconversion of energy and matter. Since energy and matter are interconvertible, and predominantly everything is energy, we cannot essentially think of destroying and uncreating any creation. However, it is possible to transform.

- Harmony is restored with the appropriateness of all that is. When everything is appropriately positioned, aligned, and oriented, harmony is restored. An example of this would be a smooth and disciplined movement of vehicles on the road.
- Healing is facilitated and experienced by all when there is harmony. Alternatively, when you heal, you re-establish harmony. When everything is in harmony, you can experience the maximum benefit from the healing.
- A resolved, aware and healed individual harmonizes and heals others in the space around him or her inadvertently. He is like a light source in a dark room. Naturally, the room will be brightened due to the sheer presence of a healed one in the space.
- A superconscious mind is aware and capable of aligning, orienting, and positioning all that is.

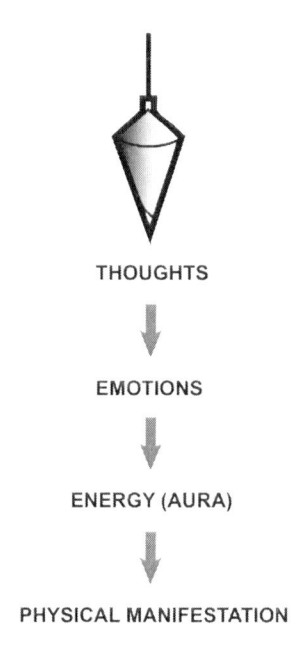

THOUGHTS
↓
EMOTIONS
↓
ENERGY (AURA)
↓
PHYSICAL MANIFESTATION

All that is, has its origin in thought.

All that is evolving, first evolves in your thoughts.

All that is transforming, first transforms in your thoughts.

Your thoughts are powerful seeds. They need to be revived or given life, their potential needs to be recognized, and they need to be realigned, reoriented, and repositioned.

Redikall Healing

Redikall Healing is an integral essence of the Redikall Insights Curriculum; brings about radical awareness of your precise thought which is manifesting or co-creating the set of experiences you are going through called life. If you wish to change the set of your experiences, you need to trace the precise causative thought.

Since all creations begin with a thought, re-creation needs re-thinking.

Your thoughts are largely influenced by the following factors:

- **Socio-economic, religious, and educational conditioning**: Your initial exposure to a set of powerful influences often shapes the way you think. For example, a child who grows up in an underprivileged environment may think differently from a child who grows up in an affluent environment.
- **Inner child**: This is the term used for a part of the personality that gets fragmented when emotional or physical traumatic experiences generate specific sets of beliefs based on the perception of the traumatic event. This can happen at any age. These beliefs eventually shape further thought processes, manifest life patterns, and invite circumstances to validate the existing beliefs. These beliefs, in turn, project and manifest corresponding circumstances and strengthen the pre-existing beliefs.
- **Preprogrammings**: You are born with certain preprogrammings that may be termed as past-life cellular memories. (Due to a different set of preprogramming, twins and triplets often display different behavioral patterns and response patterns based on their preprogramming in spite of being born under the same circumstances and astrological influence.) Preprogrammings could be experiences borrowed from lives lived by others in the past. They may remain dormant until a triggering event activates them. For example, a fear of height could be caused by a past-life preprogramming with the cellular memories of a personality who died from a fall from a great height. This memory could be triggered by a similar scene from a movie or by a visit to the peak of a mountain. These preprogrammings are strategically placed in the archive mind for a reason. Instead of removing them, they need to be decoded for the brilliance, and accept the gifts offered through them. Once we do that, the preprogramming is no longer needed and is withdrawn from actively influencing our behavior. Most phobias and certain irrational responses are based on these preprogrammings, and we shall learn to address them in the Advanced Redikall Consciousness Course.
- **Extraneous thoughts**: All thought forms that are not yours are extraneous in nature and may influence or contribute to your existing thought processes. They could be thoughts borrowed

from parents, ancestors, powerful personalities with strong beliefs, or at times dead individuals whose thoughts are still floating in your space and influencing you. Moreover, you may know them as black magic, ghosts, spirits, or negativities in common parlance. These thought forms can be metaphorically considered as germs in your space. They affect you only when you become vulnerable to them. Your vulnerability is based on certain anchoring thoughts. As your thoughts shift, the extraneous energies stop affecting you adversely. Some of the thoughts can be of great inspiration and motivation. For example, a strong parental belief in the good fortune of the child can positively shape the destiny of the child.

Thoughts are powerful.

Thoughts certainly manifest sooner or later.

If you wish to change your experience, you need to trace that exact thought and modify it to co-create and anchor the possibility of desired experience.

CHAPTER

6

Crystalline Mind: A Foundation Course for Redikall Insights

How do you heal yourself and guide others?

Healing is an ongoing process. Even if you do nothing, you are likely to be healed provided there are no obstructions to the healing process. Whenever there are traumatic events that create major dysfunctionality and disconnection with the cloud consciousness, you need to do your bit to restore the connectivity so that the healing is facilitated. You can easily heal yourself and guide others to heal themselves by applying these principles, which restore the functionality, harmony, and the experience of being *whole* once again.

"The R5: Decoded and Explained

This chapter introduces you to the application of the five "R words" that can facilitate speedy healing in a radical way.

- *Revive:* This means bringing your dormant, ignored, and unattended issues back to life. It is also powerful for inspiring the dormant part of your personality to be fully available in your present. Anything that cannot be handled by your conscious mind, and anything that appears to be extremely unpleasant or disturbing to you is likely to be stored in archive mind. Hence the dormant information, programmings and personalities need to be periodically and consistently revived so that they can be addressed appropriately.

- **Recognize:** It is important to recognize what is needed to be resolved and healed in a particular preprogramming or emotion. Recognition also enhances your awareness to enable you to be a neutral observer so you can more effectively facilitate the resolution. When you say "I recognize", the computer known as your mind runs a search for the right information that needs to be realigned, reoriented, and repositioned. Also, when you recite "I recognize", your consciousness assumes the position of a distanced observer.
- **Realign:** It is a valuable practice to align your issues to the prime resource energy or collective consciousness. When you give a command of realignment, the information that was incorrectly aligned is realigned to the prime resource energy or the higher consciousness. This information, rather than being an additional space holder, then becomes a resource for facilitating effective resolution.
- **Reorient:** Always orient your stored experiences, issues, and information in a constructive manner. When you give a command of "I reorient", the information and storage method is oriented to be constructively applicable to meet the objective set by your superconscious mind.
- **Reposition:** Position your information, associations, and experiences in appropriate spaces. When you say "I reposition", the information is positioned in such a manner that your conscious mind can easily access and use it to make it resourceful to you.

Please keep in mind, healing does not mean "fixing".

You can certainly facilitate your own healing experience.

The connectivity through realignment to the prime resource energy may naturally "fix" the perceived "flaws".

Occasionally, the perceived "flaws" may not appear to be "fixed" at the end of the healing session. In this case, you may discover the brilliance in the design and no longer see flaws as flaws. Instead, you might look at the seeming flaws as an integral part of the larger design with the higher consciousness. You will discover their appropriateness with respect to the greater good meant for all.

The magic happens by repeating Redikall Reorganization statements (refer to Appendix III) in the given sequence. These statements can be applied under various circumstances with different objectives in mind. Decide on the objective before you start healing and read out the relevant information. If you are facilitating others, you can ask them to recite these statements as well.

Discovering the Core through Onion Peeling

Your being is like an onion. As you work using these five magic Redikall "R words", you will start being consciously present to underlying issues. These issues can be of various nature. Any thought, idea, feeling, or vague memory of the past, or distracting attention to someone you met sometime back, or some sound in your environment could also be of great relevance. Pay attention to these subsequent layers and continue healing the layers until you feel totally blank and your mind feels totally at peace or experiences stillness.

You will ultimately reach a state of mind in which thoughts cease to exist. This happens when the filter mind is quite clear, and you have access to your subconscious mind as well as to the metaphysical world. If you ask a relevant question in this space, you will get a brilliant answer. At times, these answers are available to you in the form of metaphors. Examples of such metaphors are a chain loosening up, a bird flying high in the sky, light in the dark room, or a waterfall. Ask yourself a question: what does the image mean to you? You are likely to get a clear idea, a visual sign, or an audio/verbal answer. If you are working with experienced Redikall facilitators, they will guide you further in interpreting these metaphors.

Signs and Symptoms of Being Healed/Resolved

As you heal with the Redikall Foundation Technique, some of the following signs will indicate that you are being healed or resolved.

- **Breathing**: Your breathing pattern changes. You tend to breathe deeper and more rhythmically as you start healing yourself.
- **Relaxation**: Various body parts start relaxing as the number of thoughts and emotional charges are reduced.
- **Feeling sleepy**: You start feeling more and more sleepy and may attain an alpha state of mind wherein you are aware of every conversation around you and yet remain in a deep trance.
- **Releases and discharges from the body**: Bodily release happens in the form of incessant yawning, burping, coughing, sneezing, frequent urinating, and even passing gas. Discharges and gaseous release during and after healing are usually very good signs, as they make you feel lighter, refreshed, and energized. These discharges may sometimes make you feel relaxed and slightly sleepy, but they will never make you feel drained, exhausted, or tired. Excessive diarrhea, cough, cold, or fever after healing would be coincidental and may require medical consultation.
- **Feeling of vibrations and movements:** In various parts of the body based on your sensitivity and observation skills, you may experience various unusual sensations. Nostrils seem to open up, congestion in the body starts easing out. You may experience mild itching, burning, or pain which may shift from one body part to the other as you heal or resolve in layers.

- **Shifting and transient pains:** Shifting pains guide you towards the shifting thought process or emotion that needs to be addressed and resolved. Please refer to Appendix I, Keywords of Minor Chakras.
- **Changes in sleep:** After an in-depth session of very deep healing, you may feel unusually sleepy, drowsy, or laid back for a few hours to a few days. Please allow this rest phase to facilitate the reorganization of the files in your subconscious mind. The more you rest and sleep, the better and faster will you heal.
- **Changes in appetite:** Your appetite may increase or decrease depending on your body's response to the healing. Food cravings and thirst may also shift. A thorough healing can bring in a positive shift in your dietary habits.

Redikall Foundation Technique: Application and Usefulness

The simplicity and ease of using the Redikall Foundation Technique (RFT) makes it an excellent tool for addressing even our smallest concerns such as acidity, heartburn, and mild aches and pains. It also makes it an excellent tool for addressing severe concerns like insomnia, fears, and panic attacks. The following chapter discusses some of the possible applications of the RFT; however, the beauty of the modality lies in its adaptability based on the individual needs and situations. The unique onion-peeling way guides you to the core, irrespective of the method you adapt to address your concerns—direct or indirect.

Healing for Self

As you revive, recognize, realign, reorient and reposition your thoughts and emotions, you systematically resolve them and experience deeper level of healing. Regular healing can be compared to a soul-and-mind-bathing experience. As you start consistently and persistently healing yourself, you tend to have fewer thoughts and more refined emotional responses. It gets increasingly possible to remain aware of every thought and every signal from the body and do enough justice to them because you tend to be in touch with your enhanced body consciousness. You get in touch with your core, your true self, your true feelings. With regular practice, you tend to connect to the subtle signals and information that are relevant to you and your well-being. You get intuitive answers, practical solutions, creative direction, and assistance in your daily work. Decision making gets easier, and you start having a fairly good idea of the purpose of your life and your role in any given situation.

Eventually, it is you and your being that are revived, recognized, realigned, reoriented, and repositioned. You restore the harmony in your inner as well as your outer self.

Seeking Guidance, Answers, Solutions, and Directions

You can discover brilliant answers, solutions, and guidance through your subconscious mind, provided you know the art of asking the right questions and have the knowledge to design appropriate Redikall Reorganization statements. The following statements will be of immense help if you hit a dead end while healing. Keep the question in mind and recite the following statements.

> I revive my unawareness.
>
> I recognize my unawareness.
>
> I realign my unawareness.
>
> I reorient my unawareness.
>
> I reposition my unawareness.

Recite these statements seven to twenty-one times—however long it takes you to feel totally blank, at ease, or you see a comfortable metaphoric vision. You can get direct answers in a language that you understand, or you may also get a metaphoric clue. Metaphors are imaginary visual clues from the subconscious mind that present to the conscious mind certain answers, guidance, and messages over and above verbal messages. They are meant to enhance the clarity at the conscious level. If you cannot infer the answer from the clue, you can repeat the statements once again.

If you are still feeling lost and clueless, know that there is a possibility of resistance. You must address your resistance and figure out the reasons behind it (refer to Appendix III). In most such cases, you may be associating the solution, direction, or awareness with the "end", or death. Or you may be associating a state of being confused and lost with the possibility of growth. Address them with Redikall Reorganization statements and find your clues, answers, and guidance accordingly.

Redikall Foundation Technique (RFT) for Sound Sleep

Regular use of the RFT helps you to achieve sound sleep. It also reduces the number of disturbing dreams eventually. For better results, use the RFT statements for half an hour before bedtime. You can address whatever thoughts you have or any body sensations, any memories of the past, or any future concern. As you continue to address the present story, your mind will lead you from one feeling to another systematically until you feel relaxed, peaceful, and sleepy. Most people feel sleepy after reciting the statements a few times. Some people may need a bit more repetition depending on the unfolding layers.

We spend the better part of our sleeping hours processing the input we have collected throughout the day. The RFT speeds up the process; hence, we need fewer hours of sleep. We wake up refreshed in a short span of time. The need for regular use of the RFT is directly proportional to your hectic schedule.

Dynamic RFT

You can use the RFT daily in a dynamic way; for example, while traveling, waiting for the transport, taking a walk in the garden, cooking, doing mundane work like ironing, dusting, or washing dishes. It is often very difficult in your daily busy life to set aside a particular time for healing. The simple usability and applicability of the RFT relieves you from giving more priority to heal yourself over other pending tasks awaiting to be taken care by you, as you can integrate them together and multitask according to your personal discretion and capacity. A word of caution: If you have a tendency to feel sleepy while using the RFT, avoid repeating the statements while driving.

Effects of Your Inner Resolution and Healing on Others Around You

Healing yourself is a great benefit to you, but it is also a boon to people in your surroundings. As you resolve your conflicting thoughts and heal, your responses to various stimuli simultaneously change in your environment; namely, your family members, friends, and co-workers. You will observe others perceiving you at a different level, and you will see others around you shifting accordingly. People around you, pets, and even inanimate objects such as machines will respond to your healing process in a positive way. Most of the time, the following patterns are observed in and around a resolved and healed individual:

- Abusive partners change their attitude if the victimized partner heals.
- Children calm down when their parents heal themselves.
- Followers follow better when the leader heals.
- Employees respond in a better way when an employer heals.

It is far easier and prudent to heal yourself rather than helplessly and hopelessly waiting for the people around you or your situations to change. After all, everything that you see and experience around you is your own reflection and projection at some level of your existence. Thus, most of the time, Redikall Foundation Technique adopts an approach to work on your concerns and issues through yourself rather than addressing the other person, which at times is difficult due to their unavailability or disinterest in participation.

Redikall Healing Case Studies

Though Redikall Facilitators (RFs) do not claim to heal or fix or offer any alternative medicine approach, they certainly assist in decoding the reason behind complaints and aligning the seeker to the brilliance offered by the problem. With higher awareness and alignment, the healing process is facilitated. Redikall Facilitators merely guide the seeker.

Case Study 1: Pain Management with Redikall Foundation Technique

This seeker who came for a Redikall Insights Session was a thirty-five-year-old man who was complaining of a cold and cough.

Seeker: I have cough and cold.

RF: What does that make you feel?

Seeker: Stuck!

RF: Please close your eyes, breathe deeply, and scan through your body from your head to toes. Let me know where you feel this "stuck" feeling in your body.

Seeker: I did not follow that. I am feeling stuck in general in life. Because of this cold and cough, I cannot do several things.

RF: I would like you to pay close attention to your body and give me a metaphor for the stuck feeling. For example, a band or a nail stuck in the head, gases stuck in the abdomen.

Seeker: I feel as if there is a thorny bush inside my throat which I can neither swallow nor cough out.

RF: How much is the discomfort on a scale of zero to ten? Zero means you have no discomfort and ten means you have extreme discomfort.

Seeker: Five or six. [**Note:** Most people are able to give this number easily.]

RF: Now recite: I revive this thorny bush. I recognize this thorny bush. I realign this thorny bush. I reorient this thorny bush. I reposition this thorny bush. Repeat these same set of statements aloud or silently in your mind. And let me know what is happening.

Seeker [after repeating these statements]: Now the bush is not thorny, but the dry twigs are irritating the inner lining of my throat.

RF: Please repeat the following set of statements seven times: I revive these dry twigs, I recognize these dry twigs. I realign these dry twigs. I reorient these dry twigs and I reposition these dry twigs.

Seeker [after repeating these statements]: There is no thorny bush or twig, but there is a soreness like a wound, due to some abrasion which feels still open in my throat. It is as if the wound is bleeding.

RF: You can recite: I revive this bleeding wound in my throat. I recognize this bleeding wound in my throat. I realign this bleeding wound in my throat. I reorient this bleeding wound in my throat. I reposition this bleeding wound in my throat.

Seeker [after repeating these statements]: There are no wounds, but still I can see one thorn stuck in my throat.

RF: You can address the thorn in a similar way.

Seeker: I revive the thorn stuck in my throat, I recognize the thorn stuck in my throat …

RF: What is happening now?

Seeker: I see my father's face.

RF: How is this thorn associated with your father?

Seeker: As a child, when my father used to utter very critical remarks towards me, they would feel like those thorns stuck in my throat. They caused pain. I could neither swallow nor answer him back.

RF: What triggered that memory?

Seeker: My boss passed highly critical remarks on my performance in the boardroom in front of other colleagues several days ago.

RF: Okay …

Seeker: The cold and cough started right after that. I felt stuck in my job and could not leave the company because of my financial considerations. I have mortgages to clear.

RF: What is happening now?

Seeker: I am feeling better. The discomfort is almost gone, and my running nose is reduced. I have not coughed in a while.

RF: How are you going to handle your boss?

Seeker [retrieving deep thoughts]: I had an offer some time back to take a transfer to a smaller town office with a promotion. My attachment to the city life did not let me accept that offer. I think it would be a good idea to go to a smaller town, be the boss in my setup, and lead a relaxed life rather than going through constant criticism by my current boss. Actually, if not for his criticism and the way he said what he said, I would not have budged from my current job scenario. I had no clue that this cough and cold were caused by this criticism. I was thinking that my immunity was down.

RF: You were right! Certainly your immunity was down due to the stress. The cold and cough were not there to trouble you. These symptoms were merely attempting to communicate something to you. The moment you were aware of the communication from your body consciousness, you got clarity in your professional life as well. By and large, when there are no advance level pathological changes, body discomfort disappears immediately, as soon as it serves the purpose of communicating the right corrective message. Possibly a mild discomfort may remain to remind you to act based on the awareness you have received now.

Redikall case study note: This seeker had a cold and cough, which made him feel stuck. Colds and coughs can make different people feel different effects, but he chose to feel stuck. So, the RF explored the folder in which the seeker stored the feeling of being stuck. A thorny bush, dry twigs, bleeding wound, soreness, father's sharp remarks, and boss's criticism were all stored in the same folder. We simply revived, recognized, realigned, reoriented, and repositioned all of them. The files were sorted, the filter mind became clearer, and the solution present already in the subconscious mind was easily retrieved, considered, and accepted in a calmer mindset.

The Redikall Foundation Technique not only helps you in healing but also gives you relief at the emotional and physical levels. It simultaneously empowers you with an insight into higher awareness to deal with the associated situation. As you repeatedly use this technique, you can develop a highly organized information storage system in the subconscious mind, a super-refined response system, a moderated filter mind, and better awareness through metaphysical insights or through solutions available from your subconscious mind.

Case Study 2: Management of Emotions, Relationships, and the Self through the Redikall Foundation Technique

Though Redikall Facilitators (RFs) do not claim to heal or fix or offer any alternative medicine approach, they certainly assist in decoding the reason behind complaints and aligning the seeker to the brilliance offered by the problem. With higher awareness and alignment, the healing process is facilitated. Redikall Facilitators merely guide the seeker.

> This seeker who came for a Redikall Insights Session, was a young woman who was having difficulty recovering from her divorce.

Seeker [spreading hands in a gesture of helplessness]: I am not able to overcome my ex. Even after the divorce, I keep thinking of him. I feel terrible, and I cannot open up to other men because of that.

RF: What does that make you feel?

Seeker: I don't know. Maybe sad? Maybe angry? Maybe hurt? Maybe lonely? It's difficult to express. After fifteen years of companionship, he broke off as if I was a piece of shit!

RF: Take a few deep breaths … relax … and scan through your body. Where do you feel maximum discomfort?

Seeker: Chest?

RF: Inside or outside?

Seeker: Outside my chest. Here [pointing towards the middle of the chest].

RF: What do feel there?

Seeker: As if there is a big rock.

RF: Would you repeat this set of statements: I revive this big rock on my chest, I recognize this big rock on my chest. I realign this big rock on my chest. I reorient this big rock on my chest. I reposition this big rock on my chest. Let me know how you feel after repeating the statements three times each.

Seeker [after repeating these statements]: It is not so big now. It feels like a stone.

RF: Please repeat these statements: I revive this stone on my chest. I recognize this stone on my chest. I realign the stone on my chest. I reorient the stone on my chest. I reposition the stone on my chest.

Seeker: [after repeating these statements]: It's not there anymore. But I feel that there is a kind of a band around my forehead.

RF: Please repeat this seven times: I revive this band. I recognize this band. I realign this band. I reorient this band. I reposition this band.

Seeker [after repeating these statements]: I am feeling slightly lighter. I can breathe better now. Tell me, why did he do that? What did he seek in another woman? Why did he leave me for her?

RF: Kindly recite these statements: I revive my unawareness. I recognize my unawareness. I realign my unawareness. I reorient my unawareness. I reposition my unawareness.

Seeker [after repeating these statements]: Actually, our marriage came to standstill quite a while ago, before he left me. We had no sex life. I was busy with my children and job. I never bothered to ask what he wanted from me. I took him for granted. He never expressed his needs. He just vanished one fine day. I was left devastated with tears and sorrow.

RF: What does that make you feel?

Seeker [sighing and looking down]: Guilty. Very guilty for not paying enough attention to what I had. Not valuing him. I thought he did not value me. But perhaps I didn't value him. I never realized that.

RF: Where do you feel this guilt?

Seeker: In my throat. It feels like an apple core stuck in there.

RF: Please recite these statements: I revive this apple core, I recognize this apple core. I realign this apple core. I reorient this apple core. I reposition this apple core.

Seeker [after repeating these statements]: Better. What I am realizing is that I never valued myself. Why would he value me? I had taken myself for granted. I was getting burnt out and all scattered, trying to prove that I am a good teacher in the school, a good mother, a good wife, and a good daughter. I wanted to make everyone happy so that they would all value me. But I was totally burnt out, not available to myself. How could I have been available to him? [Seeker burst into tears and the RF waited for some time until the seeker calmed down.]

Seeker: Thank you! I never saw the whole scenario from that angle.

RF: Now that you have realized that you have not valued yourself, what are you planning to do about it?

Seeker: I realize that I need to value and respect myself. But I do not know how to do that. I have not done that ever in my life.

RF: Recite these statements: I revive my unawareness. I recognize my unawareness. I realign my unawareness. I reorient my unawareness. I reposition my unawareness.

Seeker [after repeating these statements]: I chose to consult you because I valued him and wanted him back. But what I needed was to have myself back with me. I am not myself. I am what others wanted me to be. How can I do that? Can you guide me?

RF: Sure. We can address that in subsequent sessions. However, you can start practicing what I have taught you. These statements will give you deeper and deeper insights. You will be able to sort out most of the issues. You will be able to see your relationship with yourself, with others, with your body, and with the world in a different way and in a different light. You will be able to get answers to your questions on your own, and if you still do not, we can schedule additional sessions.

Seeker: Thank you so much! I realize that I actually had to lose him to find myself. Though I have not totally found myself yet, I am sure with this awareness and some more effort, I will get a new direction in life. Looking back in life and waiting for him is meaningless. Let me now see how I can do the best for myself! Thank you so much. You have touched my soul somewhere.

Redikall case study note: As it was with this case study, many times people want to fix something outside them. A Redikall Healing consultant brings in an awareness by assisting them to see their scenarios with Redikall insight. Most of the seekers cannot believe that it can be so simple, fast, and easy. How can it be practically a "no-fuss" technique? How can someone help you out without you describing the issues and concerns as this case history details? Let us show you the way it works.

The Redikall Foundation Technique, which I use today, cuts therapeutic efforts short. Results are achieved in a considerably short period of time. Though the RFT is not meant to replace any therapeutic modality, you can always complement it with any existing therapeutic modalities. Though I do not practice homeopathy and hypnotherapy now, I wish I had known this technique earlier. I would have been able to understand my clients in a better way had I known the Redikall Foundation Technique.

CHAPTER

7

Steps in the Redikall Foundation Technique

This chapter introduces you to the Redikall Foundation Technique for keeping your filter mind clear, reorganizing various information and stored experiences in your subconscious mind, and storing them in appropriate folders. The technique is followed by the explanation of the keywords used for healing.

The process is as follows:

Step 1: Identify an issue or a feeling as experienced by you or your seeker.

Step 2: Give an intensity to that issue or feeling on a scale of zero to ten (zero means that the intensity of the issue is not there at all, and ten means that the intensity of the issue is at its maximum).

Step 3: Repeat the following statements. Replace the asterisks with the issue or feeling you wish to explore.

> I revive *****.
>
> I recognize *****.
>
> I realign *****.

I reorient *****.

I reposition *****.

I revive: When you cannot handle situations, emotions, or experiences, you often tend to benumb yourself and bury the issues deep within your tissues or in your archive mind. They become dead memories or experiences for you. Because you are unable to address them effectively without going through the associated pains all over again, you perhaps choose to be indifferent to them or to deny them, making them dormant. Repeated recital—silently or aloud—of the Redikall Reorganization statements enables you to get in touch with those dormant memories or bring them to the surface to resolve and eventually heal them: I revive my grief, I revive my hurt, I revive my rejection, I revive my pain, I revive my disease. However, saying this statement can be a little uncomfortable to begin with for some people; yet it is necessary. If you continue to feel uneasy, do not force yourself to recite the "I revive" statement. Continue with the remaining statements and keep repeating them until you feel comfortable reciting "I revive …".

I recognize: In order to recognize anything or anyone, you need to be in the position of an observer. When you say "I recognize", you are emotionally and consciously distancing yourself enough to be able to neutrally observe yourself, your responses, your issues, and others around you. For example: I recognize my stored grief, I recognize my hurts, I recognize my pain, I recognize my disease. Statements like these enable you to raise your consciousness and become a neutral observer to your own pain, grief, disease, or related issues. Remember, as Albert Einstein said, "No problem can be solved from the same level of consciousness that created it." Therefore, in order to recognize any affliction, you need to raise your consciousness to bring it to your cognizance.

I realign: You realign yourself to the resources freely available to you. There is a constant flow of resources, wisdom, and brilliance. You could be having a problem due to nonalignment with the resources. Therefore, as and when you choose to realign, you will easily be able to take advantage of them. The greatest resource is the healing energy. When you align correctly, you enable the healing energy to purify, heal, integrate, and protect various parts of your personality.

I reorient: With this step, you are asked to reorient yourself in your feelings, beliefs, emotional responses, energies, and your approach to all that is, including your approach towards your own self. Everything in the world is ultimately a form of energy. The energy cannot be destroyed, but it can be oriented and channeled to your advantage.

I reposition: While repositioning, you are requested to give the right position to yourself, others, all your feelings, all your beliefs, and all your relationships—all that is you and belongs to you, as there is a brilliance in all that is. However, even the most brilliant asset, if not positioned correctly, can be meaningless for you. Even if you have seemingly unproductive waste materials or concepts, correctly positioning them will make them meaningful to you or others in your universe.

The Aha! moments you experience after reciting appropriate Redikall Reorganization Statements are the end results of a clear filter mind and realigned, reoriented, and repositioned information in various folders of the subconscious mind, which enables an exchange of precious information from and through the subconscious mind.

Part 2
Healing Recipes for Mind Management

CHAPTER

8

Healing through the Redikall Foundation Technique

With the Redikall Foundation Technique, you can address multiple issues and concerns in your life.

(1) Heal Physical and Emotional Pains

What is pain?

The International Association for the Study of Pain (https://www.iasp-pain.org/Taxonomy#Pain) defines pain as "An unpleasant sensory or emotional experience associated with actual or potential tissue damage or described in terms of such damage."

Therefore, pain is an unpleasant experience. It can be physical or emotional in nature and essentially is a warning signal that tells you that, if nothing is done about it, there is a risk of further damage.

Metaphysically, "PAIN" indicates the need to "Pay Attention to Information Now". This information may be from the body consciousness. Pain is one of the ways in which your body communicates with you and gives you vital clues you can use to enhance your awareness of an awesome life experience.

Pain in certain body parts can fairly well give you the knowledge of corresponding erroneous thought processes that need to be corrected. When you correct the thinking, you get instant relief from the pain.

Redikall Facilitators (RF) treat your pain by providing you with deeper insights. They are trained through the Essential Redikall Insights Course and the Advanced Courses for Redikall Insights curriculum. They know that every pain has a message for you. The pain will persist only until you decode the intended message and apply it to enhance your life. This theory does not apply to the pain caused by structural changes such as tumor, cancer, fracture or advanced Osteoarthritis. In above cases, the reversal may or may not happen soon even though occasionally pain reduces considerably.

Addressing Physical and Emotional Pain

With Redikall Foundation Technique, physical pains are best healed at an emotional level and emotional pains are best healed at physical level.

For example, if you are experiencing a headache, ask yourself, "How does this pain make me feel?" Address the headache by addressing the accompanied feeling with Redikall Reorganization statements.

On the other hand, if you are feeling angry, you may ask, "Where in the body do I feel this anger?" Then address the body sensation, and you will be easily addressing your anger through bodily sensations. For example, anxiety can be felt in the belly like a knot in the intestines. When you address the knot in the intestine, the level of anxiety begins to reduce too.

Emotional pains are felt in layers, and they may also create various sensations in the physical body. Body sensations may be felt in the form of aches, pains, discomforts, heaviness, numbness, stiffness, vibration, sensation, growling, pinching, weight, tingling, itchiness, and so forth. Thus, when experiencing an emotional pain, be open and aware of the changing sensations in your body. For example, when experiencing anger, anxiety, or sadness, you may directly address it at the level of the emotion, working through it layer by layer till the time you experience inner silence and stillness within. The thoughtless mind and painless body will indicate that you have done enough work for the time being. In this state of being, you will get the right answers, solutions, and directions.

When you achieve a state of thoughtless mind and painless body, you can ask the right questions to yourself to get right answers, solutions and directions.

Alternatively, focus on the discomfort that the emotion creates in your body, heal that discomfort, and thereby heal the emotional pain. You may not be accustomed to recognizing your emotions or feelings or their effect on various parts of your body. In this case, address whatever comes to your mind and keep scanning your body for different sensations. Once you start getting in touch with the sensations, you focus on them instead of the causative emotions.

Redikall note: If you have the knowledge of Essential Redikall Insights Course, you may keep in mind the corresponding metaphysical message from the body and integrate that with your Redikall Reorganization Statements. Though Redikall can magically assist you in pain management, we recommend you consult your physician to rule out deeper pathology and surgical need if any.

If you are yet to learn about this, you can still help yourself and guide others fairly well using the Keywords of Minor Chakras (refer to Appendix I) and the Redikall Reorganization Statements (refer to Appendix III).

Physical Pain

Though you can address your pain directly, for faster results, consider addressing emotions associated with the pain on a priority basis:

Step 1: Focus your attention on the specific location where you experience physical pain in the body.

Step 2: Rate this pain on a scale of zero to ten (zero means you have absolutely no pain, and ten means you are experiencing extreme, excruciating pain).

Step 3: Recite the following statements aloud or silently in your mind seven to twenty-one times.

- I revive my pain.
- I recognize my pain.
- I realign my pain.
- I reorient my pain.
- I reposition my pain.

Or, for example, if you have back pain, the Redikall Reorganization statements would be:

- I revive my back pain.
- I recognize my back pain.
- I realign my back pain.
- I reorient my back pain.
- I reposition my back pain.

Redikall note: You may refer to Appendix III, Redikall Reorganization statements, and make your Redikall Reorganization statements by replacing ***** with "pain" or "pain in ######" where ##### represents the precise body part.

Redikall note: If you need further assistance, you may connect to a Redikall Facilitator or a Redikall Mentor.

Step 4: Now reassess the intensity of the pain to evaluate your current level of discomfort. Rate your discomfort and pain once more on a scale of zero to ten as before. These are the following possibilities:

- **You are pain free:** You feel totally fine, and your pain is completely gone. In this case, you can choose to work with another issue if you wish to or simply celebrate your pain-free existence.
- **Your pain is reduced:** You feel slightly better but not yet totally fine. In this case, you can recite your statements a few more times until you are pain free. For chronic pains (for example, arthritis or

certain structural changes in joints) you may need to recite daily for up to three months.

- **Your pain is better; however, another issue has come to your awareness or the pain has shifted its location to somewhere else in your body:** You are advised to repeat the first set of statements where you replace ***** with the new pain or discomfort. For example, the pain shifts from your back to your knee. Recite:

  - I revive my knee pain.
  - I recognize my knee pain.
  - I realign my knee pain.
  - I reorient my knee pain.
  - I reposition my knee pain.

- **The pain is the same:** There is a possibility of structural change causing the pain. In such a case, you may have to recite the Redikall Reorganization statements for twenty-one to ninety days. If there are no known structural changes and the pain remains the same or has increased, there could be a possibility of a subconscious resistance to recover. In this case, use the following statements.

  - I revive my resistance to be free from this pain.
  - I recognize my resistance to be free from this pain.
  - I realign my resistance to be free from this pain.
  - I reorient my resistance to be free from this pain.
  - I reposition my resistance to be free from this pain.

Alternatively, you can use the second set of statements where you replace ***** with the issue, pain, or discomfort you are healing.

Step 5: Reassess the level of pain once more on a scale of zero to ten as before. Ensure that the pain is at level zero—you are totally pain free. If it is not, ask yourself or the person you are guiding, "How does this pain make you feel?" For example: A person may feel helpless or uncomfortable or worried or handicapped due to this pain.

When you address the associated emotions, you indirectly address the physical issue as well due to shared storage folder in your subconscious mind.

Emotional aspect of Pain – address emotions related to physical pain

Step 6: Work towards addressing the emotion generated by the pain in order to address the physical pain. Interestingly, as you work with the emotion, it's likely that the pain will shift or be considerably reduced. However, you may need to work with several layers of emotions in a sequence for substantial relief.

Step 7: Identify the emotions associated with the pain. For example, your pain may be making you feel angry, vulnerable, irritable, or anxious. In general, when addressing any emotional pain, you may think about, recall, or imagine people, situations, events, and experiences that make you feel that emotion right now or have made you feel it in the past.

Step 8: Assess the intensity of that emotion within you on a scale of zero to ten (zero means you have absolutely no such emotion or intensity, and ten means you have extremely high emotional charge).

Step 9: Repeat first set of statements by replacing ***** with the emotion you are feeling. You may make it specific if necessary; for example, knee pain is making you feel angry. The pain initially started because your father yelled at you today. For example:

- I revive my anger.
- I recognize my anger.
- I realign my anger.
- I reorient my anger.
- I reposition my anger.

Or

- I revive my anger because my father yelled at me.
- I recognize my anger because my father yelled at me.
- I realign my anger because my father yelled at me.

- I reorient my anger because my father yelled at me.
- I reposition my anger because my father yelled at me.

Step 10: Again, reassess the intensity of your emotional pain. Rate your pain once more on a scale of zero to ten as before. The same possibilities as before apply here too.

- **You feel totally fine:** Your emotional pain is completely gone. In this case, you can choose to work with another emotion if you wish to or simply celebrate your pain free existence.
- **Your emotional pain is reduced:** You feel slightly better but not yet totally fine. In this case, you can recite the statement a few more times until you feel calm and at ease.
- **Your emotional pain is better; however, another layer of emotion has come to your awareness:** You are advised to repeat the first set of statements where you replace ***** with the new emotion. For example: After anger, the next layer of emotion that surfaces could be a feeling of helplessness, then hurt and so on.
  - I revive my helplessness.
  - I recognize my helplessness.
  - I realign my helplessness.
  - I reorient my helplessness.
  - I reposition my helplessness.
  - I revive my hurt.
  - I recognize my hurt.
  - I realign my hurt.
  - I reorient my hurt.
  - I reposition my hurt.
- **The emotional pain is same or has increased:** This suggests a subconscious resistance to recover. You can use the second set of statements where you replace ***** with the emotion you are healing. For example:
  - I revive my resistance to be free from this anger.
  - I recognize my resistance to be free from this anger.

- I realign my resistance to be free from this anger.
- I reorient my resistance to be free from this anger.
- I reposition my resistance to be free from this anger.

Step 11: Reassess the level of emotional pain once more on a scale of zero to ten as before. Ensure that the pain is at level zero—you feel totally pain free, calm, and at ease.

Please note:

- You may address a physical pain by identifying somatic—or bodily—sensations one by one and working through them. At any point in time, you may shift to the emotions associated with that pain and address that emotion. Similarly, you may address emotional pain at the level of the emotions, working through them layer by layer. Again, at any point in time, you may shift to address the body sensations associated with that emotion. Therefore, you may choose to move back and forth between addressing body sensations and the emotions you feel.
- When working with body discomfort and sensations for addressing the emotions, you may also work with specific keywords associated with that body part. Refer to the keywords for minor chakras in Appendix I.
- It is a good idea to always repeat the statements a minimum of three times for each set of statements or until you feel no more pain or other sensations in the body and you feel at ease.
- Relief from the pain and discomfort is a by-product of Redikall Facilitation. The objective of the pain management is to know yourself through your pain and resolve your inner issues, conflicts and emotional blocks to make a positive difference in your life. Pain is a reminder to address what is unresolved within you. As you raise your consciousness, you rise beyond your need for inner resolution through pains and discomfort. You figure out better ways to recognize 'self' with ease and peace.

Physical pain may not respond appropriately to the Redikall Foundation Technique under following circumstances:

- Advanced structural changes such as fracture, tumor, bony growth, or osteoarthritis may not respond.
- A person has not grasped the message through the pain.
- A person has a need to learn through pain.
- A person fears being pain free (possibly fearing the duties, work, or responsibilities that must be faced when the pain is gone).
- A person does not believe in the modality. In such case, you can work with revive, recognize, realign, reorient, and reposition the doubts or disbelief.
- A person suffers from guilt from giving physical pain to others.
- A person needs to punish himself or herself.
- A person has a strong positive association of growth through pain.
- A person believes that pains are a part and parcel of life.
- A person believes that pain is one of the ways to be closer to God or spirituality.

(2) Heal Fears, Anxieties, and Phobias

What are fears, anxieties, and phobias?

The fear mechanism is meant to aid our effective survival. However, excessive fear often becomes counterproductive in nature.

> ***Fear is the end result of lack of preparedness to accept all that is.***
>
> ***The aware acceptance reduces the need for fear.***

Depending upon the level of your personal and spiritual growth, various causative factors can give you fear. Fear can develop about situations most people would consider severe, such as loss of life (yours or others), and it can develop about situations most people would consider trivial, such as missing a movie show.

Here are some examples of common fears:

- A possible threat of loss of life, material possessions, and finances.
- The possibility of going through pain.
- The possibility of losing control.
- The possibility of hurt in a friendship, romantic or other relationship.
- The possibility of losing confidence or honor.
- The possibility of not being able to implement dreams, ideas, and visions.
- The possibility of disconnection with the source or the divine.

You can address the fear by reducing the emotional charge that is the result of fear.

When the emotional charge is reduced, clarity prevails, and the aware acceptance of the outcome is facilitated.

Fear can be triggered by many important circumstances. These make people hold onto their fear making it more difficult to address.

- There is usually a subconscious preprogramming of the guilt of making others feel scared or misusing courage in the past. Therefore, this is the first aspect that needs to be addressed.
- If you have been preprogrammed with guilt of making others feel fearful and cowardly, you may choose to experience fear at your subconscious or soul level.
- Look at the possibility of an association of fear with security and care from authority—parental figures, loved ones, or God—which must be addressed. For example, a fearful sibling gets away with more concessions and kindness compared to a courageous one.
- Many people believe that courageous and bold people are loners, that fear attracts companionship, or fear keeps them safe in this world. It is, therefore, important to address these beliefs.

- Most people cope with fear through hoarding, collecting, or creating safety nets at various levels. It would be advisable to address these too.
- Focus on subconscious agenda for clinging on to the fear.

It is helpful to consider these factors while designing statements.

Finally, the emotion of fear can be addressed at both general and specific levels.

When the emotional charge of fear reduces to level zero, clarity prevails, and it is important to focus on clarity and design the statements based on clarity for reinforcement in the subconscious mind for long-term fear management.

Anxiety is an emotional response to perceived uncertainties in outcome. It arises out of a strong desire to do something or achieve a certain outcome, which appears to be beyond one's control and uncertain in nature. At times there is an association of anxiety and concern with love, especially if a parent or grandparent figure has demonstrated worry and anxiety as he or she expressed loving concern for you.

Phobia is an irrational fear of situations, objects, people, or animals. One cannot logically explain the reason behind these extreme fearful responses. For example, some people fear spiders, and others fear open spaces.

Individuals suffering from phobias often regress to past lives where there was an association of death with the factors that trigger present-life phobic responses. For example, a person suffering from a fear of heights often regresses to a past life where he or she died because of a fall from a height. Interestingly, after the regression work and healing, the person recovers instantly.

We will learn about regression work in the Advanced Redikall Consciousness Course. It is advisable not to deal with phobias at the Redikall Crystalline Mind and Essential Redikall Healing Course levels of expertise and knowledge.

Fears, anxieties, and phobias can be dealt at two levels:

- The mind level: This is where the reaction is initiated.
- The somatic level: This is where the response to the perceived threat or uncertainties is experienced in the body (body sensations, pain, and discomfort).

Follow these steps when addressing fear:

1) Determine if the fear is acute at the moment or if it is a chronic issue. If it is acute in nature, you can skip steps 2–6 and start with number 7. Once fear is reasonably settled or almost reduced to a minimum, you can address your fear with the tips mentioned in steps 2–6.
2) Address the subconscious preprogramming of fear; for example, the guilt of frightening others or misusing courage in the past. Repeat the first set of Redikall Reorganization Statements (refer to Appendix III) by replacing ***** with "my guilt of frightening others in the past", "my guilt of misusing courage in the past", or similar appropriate feelings which need to be addressed.
3) Address the association of fear. Replace ***** in the statements with "my association of fear with security from God", "my association of fear with care", or similar appropriate feelings which need to be addressed.
4) Address the beliefs related to fear. Replace ***** in the statements with "my belief that courageous and bold people are loners", "my belief that fear attracts companionship", "my belief that fear gives safety", or similar appropriate feelings which need to be addressed.
5) Address the coping methods related to fear. Replace ***** in the statements with "my need to cope with fear through hoarding or collecting", "my need to cope with fear through the creation of safety nets at various levels in my life" or similar appropriate feelings which need to be addressed.
6) Now, address the general or specific fear. Think of the subject or person or another trigger which normally gives you fear or anxiety.

For example, you may fear enclosed spaces, dogs, taking exams, or speaking in public.
7) Feel that fear in your body. This is the somatic sensation of fear. Identify where in the body it is causing any kind of pain, discomfort, sensation, or vibration. What is this sensation like?

In order to trace this discomfort correctly, ask yourself some probing questions in the following manner: Where do I feel fear or anxiety in my body, and how does it feel in that part of the body? Do I feel it in my head? Neck? Chest? Abdomen? Limbs?

For example, if the answer is "the abdomen", ask the next question: What am I feeling in my abdomen? If the answer that comes is "some pull", ask: What is being pulled? If the answer that comes is "my guts are being pulled", ask further: What is pulling my guts? If the answer that comes is "two strings", in your mind, these strings are the metaphor for something that is causing uncertainties, lack of control, and probable threat to you. You can cut short the therapeutic efforts if you address the strings rather than your fears.

8) Rate this body sensation of fear on a scale of zero to ten (zero means you have absolutely no somatic discomfort or sensation of fear, and ten means you are experiencing extreme or excruciating somatic discomfort or sensation of fear).
9) Recite the first set of statements, replacing ***** with a specific fear or anxiety related to the discomfort you are feeling in your body. For example, replace the ***** in the statements by the word "these strings" or "I revive these two strings pulling my guts". Other examples might be a heavy ball in the skull, a knot in the stomach, knife-like pain in the chest, smoke in the chest, or a boulder on the back.
10) Reassess the feeling of fear again on a scale of zero to ten as before. If the rating is still more than zero, keep repeating the statements.
11) Be open and aware of the changing body sensations and recite accordingly. As with the example I have given here, if you feel

growling in your stomach, replace ***** with "the growling in my stomach" in the statements.

12) When working with body discomfort and sensations for addressing the emotions, you may also work with specific keywords associated with that body part. Refer Appendix I, Keywords for Minor Chakras.

It is a good idea to always repeat the statements a minimum of three times for each set of statements or until you feel no more pain or other sensations in the body and you feel at ease.

Redikall Note: Fears are meant to help us survive. Fear may persist in a dormant form until you learn to operate out of complete awareness. As the level of awareness enhances, the need for the fear reduces. Fear is the subconscious mind's defense mechanism. Rather than eliminating the fear, you need to learn to make the best use of fear by easing response and gaining the insights offered by the fear.

(3) Heal Anger

What is anger?

Anger is essentially an aggressive response to perceived unpleasantness. When people feel out of control, they may become angry. They may suppress this anger or express it in an outburst.

The causative factors behind anger and the resulting responses to anger often indicate a person's level of personal and spiritual growth. We should attempt to embrace and accept the level of spiritual growth and focus on shifting to the next level because evolution is the norm of life.

Reasons for Anger

- Threat of loss of life (one's own or one's loved ones) or loss of material possessions
- Physical or emotional pains and hurts

- Perception of loss of control
- Hurt by loved ones
- Adverse effect on self-esteem, self-confidence, and self-belief
- Adverse effect on implementation of dreams, ideas, and vision
- Feeling of alienation from the divine

Responses Associated with Anger

- Taking destructive, life threatening, physically violating, homicidal, or suicidal actions
- Emotionally hurting and destabilizing others or self (emotional blackmailing, taunting, criticizing, pressing a person's buttons, emotionally triggering)
- Controlling others through anger
- Feeling of rejection and indifference, emotional disconnection
- Humiliating and dishonoring others or self
- Sabotaging plans, progress or projects in general. Manipulating at metaphysical level (tantra, black magic, soul-level curses, occult sciences)
- Feeling anger and wrath towards creation and the Creator. Sabotaging life purpose in general

Anger may not fully disappear. However, you can work towards refining the response. Check your response pattern and identify the positive factor. Know that everything is appropriate if your responses are correctly aligned, oriented, and positioned with aware and constructive intent behind your response.

Anger is not necessarily a negative emotion. Misdirected anger, for sure, can be a disadvantage. Rather than rejecting anger or ignoring anger, it is advisable to revive, recognize, realign, reorient, and reposition the stored anger. In short, if you can not address your anger, at least learn to apply it constructively with higher consciousness.

Anger carries a great amount of energy. Often a person without anger feels very vulnerable because anger is so often used as a defense mechanism.

While resolving your anger, be assured that it is possible to feel safe both with and without anger.

Important Factors about Anger

There are many important situations that generate anger. Anger can be merely the tip of an iceberg. Several emotions are generated before we feel anger. The most common ones are frustration, helplessness, powerlessness, and intimidation.

- There is a possibility of subconscious preprogramming of extreme helplessness, hopelessness, cowardly and meek behavior in the past; therefore, this is the first aspect that needs to be addressed.
- Many times, there can be an association of anger with strength and power, and this must be addressed.
- It is a common belief that people harm you or take advantage of you if you do not show your anger; for example: anger makes others obey you, nobody complies until you get angry, anger is a professional asset, anger generates respect, people take me seriously only when I demonstrate anger, or nothing gets done till I get angry. It is, therefore, important to address these beliefs.
- Many people hold onto their fears related to anger such as fear of people taking them for granted, fear of people not respecting them, or fear of being hurt or damaged in the absence of anger. These fears must be addressed before working on the actual anger.
- Most people cope with anger by suppressing it and directing it to their tissues. It is advisable to take up physical exercises or engage in rigorous physical activities to release anger.

It is helpful to consider these factors while designing statements.

Finally, the emotion of anger can be addressed at both general and specific levels.

It is important to let people know that it is possible to constructively achieve results while in a calm state of mind.

Uncontrolled expressions of anger can be compared to alcoholic binges, which may give a person a 'high' but is likely to be followed by uneasiness and low feeling soon after the effects of temporary 'high' wane.

Do not aim at rejecting anger; rather, aim at realigning, reorienting, and repositioning anger so that it benefits you and everyone around you.

Addressing Chronic Anger

If you are experiencing acute or very recent anger issues, it would be a good idea to start addressing them from step 8 onwards. Later, at your convenience, follow the entire sequence of steps.

1) Address the subconscious preprogramming of extreme helplessness and hopelessness, cowardly and meek behavior in the past. Repeat the first set of Redikall Reorganization statements (refer to Appendix III) by replacing ***** with "my cowardice", "my meek behavior", "my helplessness", "my hopelessness", "my frustration", or similar appropriate feelings which need to be addressed.
2) Address the association of anger. Replace ***** in the statements with "my association of anger with strength", "my association of anger with power". If you had a role model who used to display anger often, you may subconsciously imitate that person. You may demonstrate overt anger to feel as strong and powerful as your role model.
3) Address the belief related to anger. Replace ***** in the statements with "my belief that people harm me or take advantage of me if I do not show my anger", "my belief that anger makes others obey me", "my belief that nobody complies until I get angry", "my belief that anger is a professional asset", "my belief that anger gives me respect", "my belief that people take me seriously only when I demonstrate anger", "my belief that nothing gets done till I get angry", or similar appropriate beliefs which need to be addressed.
4) Address the fears related to anger. Replace ***** in the statements with "my fear of people taking me for granted", "my fear of people

not respecting me", "my fear of being damaged if anger is gone", or similar appropriate feelings which need to be addressed.

5) Address suppressed anger: Replace ***** in the statements with "my suppressed anger".

6) Now address the general or specific anger. Think about, recall, or imagine people, situations, events, and experiences that make you feel angry right now or have made you angry in the past. Assess the extent of feeling within you on a scale of zero to ten (zero means you have absolutely no anger, and ten means you have extremely high anger).

7) Repeat both sets of Redikall Reorganization statements by replacing ***** with "my anger". You may make it specific, if necessary; for example, replace ***** with "my anger at losing my job", "my anger at being yelled at by my father", or "my anger at myself".

8) Reassess the feeling on a scale of zero to ten as before. If the rating is still more than zero, repeat the statements. Be open and aware of the next layer of emotions and recite accordingly. Replace ***** with, say, "my anger at losing my job", "my helplessness because of loss of my job", or "my hurt and betrayal because my colleague conspired against me and made me lose my job".

9) It is important to address the somatic—or bodily—sensations associated with the emotion of anger. You may ask yourself, "Where do I feel this anger in my body right now?" You may feel, say, any ache or pain, discomfort, heaviness, numbness, stiffness, vibration, sensation, growling, pinching, weight, tingling, or itchiness in your body.

10) Assess that sensation in your body on a scale of zero to ten (zero means you have absolutely no sensation in the body, and ten means you have extreme sensation in the body). Repeat both sets of Redikall Reorganization statements, replacing ***** with the respective sensations in the body that you experience. Be open and aware of the changing body sensations and recite accordingly. For example, you sense anger in your right bicep in the form of a pinching pain. Replace ***** with "the pinching pain in my right bicep". Then, if your body sensations for anger changes and you

start to feel burden on your shoulders, replace ***** with "the burden on my shoulders" in the statements.

When working with body discomfort and sensations for addressing the emotions, you may also work with specific keywords associated with that body part. Refer to Appendix I, Keywords for Minor Chakras.

Redikall note: The 250+ minor chakras are explained in the Essential Redikall Insights Course.

It is a good idea to always repeat the statements a minimum of three times for each set of statements or until there is no more pain or other sensations in the body and you feel at ease.

(4) Heal Helplessness

What is helplessness?

All humans enjoy a fair level of control over themselves, situations, and people around them.

However, it is not always possible to do what you wish to do, to receive what you wish to receive, to command what you would like to command. This results in a helpless feeling because you do not find yourself or anybody else able to help you in a given situation.

Helplessness makes you feel like a victim, and if you already have a victim mindset, then you may experience helplessness quite frequently.

Being a victim or a victimizer along with helplessness and adversities are intricately interwoven experiences. People may think that helplessness is the end result of adversity. However, a need for helplessness may manifest adversities.

In a similar way, the victim may feel victimized because of the victimizer. However, the attitude of the victimizer could be the result of the victim's need to be victimized.

We have clinically found that, when a victim or a helpless person chooses to realign, reorient, and reposition his or her needs and experiences, adversities offer added benefit, and the victimizer transforms his or her approach towards the victim.

It is important to stop expecting the external environment and other people to change. Instead, focus on manifesting a constructive shift in your perception, attitude, and response system.

Important Factors about Helplessness

There are many important aspects that work behind helplessness. These make people hold onto this emotion, making it difficult to address.

- You could be having a subconscious preprogramming of victimizing and making others feel victimized in the past. Therefore, this is the first aspect that needs to be addressed.
- Often there is an association of helplessness with receiving extra favors, sympathy, and attention, which must be addressed.
- Many people believe that, in order to feel better, other people, situations, and environmental factors have to shift, and being helpless brings one closer to God. It is, therefore, important to address these beliefs.
- Many people hold onto their fears related to the freedom from helplessness, such as fear of becoming a tyrant, fear of being arrogant, fear of making others feel helpless, and fear of victimizing others. These fears must be addressed before working on the actual helplessness.
- Most people cope with helplessness by showing aggression and anger, implementing various kinds of defenses, portraying extra powers, or attempting to be independent. It is important to address these defense mechanisms too.

Reasons behind Helplessness

- Loss or threat to material possessions
- Pain, hurt, or the possibility of being hurt
- Loss of control or power
- Rejection, abandonment, or bereavement
- Loss of prestige, misunderstanding, blame, guilt, humiliation, social embarrassment, or shame
- Inability to realize the dreams or do what you wish to do
- A perceived sense of distance from the divine

Evolutionary Response towards Helplessness

- Experiencing suicidal tendencies, a lack of desire to live, waiting for death
- Entertaining, overindulging in, or escaping in pleasurable activities including sex, food, shopping, or traveling
- Attempting to control all that can be controlled, displaying bouts of anger, being irritable, indulging in temper tantrums
- Hurting, holding grudges, and attempting to wall off that which is not desired
- Needing to express or gain sympathy from others; gaining attention from others
- Making the best out of helplessness and turning helpless experiences into personal favor; for example, gaining mass sympathy for being victimized and leading a social movement to uplift other victims
- Having insight into your manifestation of being a victimizer and victimizing situation. Discovering the brilliance in the divine plan

Finally, the emotion of helplessness can be addressed at both general and specific levels—acute or chronic.

Addressing Helplessness

If there you are experiencing acute feelings of helplessness, you can skip points 1–8 and start with point 9.

1) Address the subconscious preprogramming of victimizing and making others feel victimized in the past. Repeat the first set of Redikall Reorganization statements (refer to Appendix III) by replacing ***** with "my guilt of victimizing and making others feel victimized in the past".
2) Address the association of helplessness. Replace ***** in the statements with "my association of helplessness with extra favours, sympathy and attention", or similar feelings and associations.
3) Address the belief related to helplessness. Replace ***** in the statements with "my belief that, in order to feel better, others, my situations, and my environment have to shift", "my belief that being helpless brings me closer to God", or similar feelings that need to be addressed.
4) Address the fears related to helplessness. Replace ***** in the statements with "my fear of becoming a tyrant", "my fear of being arrogant", "my fear of making others feel helpless", "my fear of victimising others", or similar fears that need to be addressed.
5) Address coping mechanisms of helplessness. Replace ***** in the statements with "my aggression and anger", "my defences of helplessness", "my need to portray extra powers", or "my attempt to be independent".
6) Now address the general or specific helplessness. Think about, recall, or imagine people, situations, events, and experiences that make you feel helpless right now or have made you feel helpless in the past. Assess the extent of that feeling within you on a scale of zero to ten (zero means you have absolutely no emotional charge related to helplessness, and ten means you have extremely high emotional charge related to helplessness).
7) Repeat both sets of Redikall Reorganization statements by replacing ***** with "my helplessness". You may make it specific, if necessary; for example, replace ***** with, say, "my helplessness at losing my job" or "my helplessness at being bullied by my brother".
8) Reassess the emotional charge again on a scale of zero to ten as before. If the rating is still more than zero, repeat the statements. Be open and aware of the next layer of emotions and recite

accordingly. Replace ***** with, say, "my helplessness at losing my job", "my hurt at losing my job", or "my grief at losing my job".

9) It is important to address the somatic—or bodily—sensations associated with the emotion of helplessness too. You may ask yourself, "Where do I feel this helplessness in my body right now?" You may feel, say, any ache or pain, discomfort, heaviness, numbness, stiffness, vibration, sensation, growling, pinching, weight, tingling, or itchiness in your body.

10) Assess that sensation in your body on a scale of zero to ten (zero means you have absolutely no sensation in the body, and ten means you have extreme sensation in the body). Repeat both sets of Redikall Reorganization statements by replacing ***** with the respective sensations in the body as you experience. Be open and aware of the changing body sensations and recite accordingly.

For example, you sense helplessness in your right elbow in the form of a striking pain. Replace ***** with "the striking pain in my right elbow". If your body sensation for helplessness changes and you start feeling pain on your right forearm, replace ***** with "the pain on my right forearm" in the statements.

11) When working with body discomfort and sensations for addressing the emotions, you may also work with specific keywords associated with that body part. Refer to Appendix I, Keywords for Minor Chakras.

Redikall note: The 250+ minor chakras are explained in the Essential Redikall Insights Course.

It is a good idea to always repeat the statements a minimum of three times for each set of statements or until you feel no more pain or sensation in the body and you feel at ease.

(5) *Heal Hopelessness*

What is hopelessness?

Hope is that lubricant which helps you glide over seemingly rough patches in life. When you lose touch with hope, the situation appears harsher and more difficult, coping up becomes a big challenge, and adverse feelings grip your life.

Hope is a basic requirement for most people.

Reasons for Hopelessness

- Terminal disease or life-threatening situation
- Unbearable and unresolved pain
- Persistent lack of control over life or people around
- Repeated hurts from loved ones
- Persistent lack of confidence and low self-esteem
- Constant difficulties in implementations
- Disconnection from the divine

Evolutionary Response towards Hopelessness

- Having suicidal thoughts or ideas
- Wanting to escape into pleasurable stimuli as often as possible
- Wanting to create boundaries and be unapproachable by other members of the society
- Attempting to wall up and remain unavailable to loved ones to prevent further rejection
- Avoiding social and social media interaction and communication
- Being lethargic and adopting a laid-back attitude
- Disbelieving in and disconnecting from the divine

Important Factors about Hopelessness

There are many important aspects that anchor the experience of hopelessness. These make people hold onto this emotion, and this makes it difficult to address.

- There is a subconscious preprogramming of guilt of making others hopeless in the past. Therefore, this is the first aspect that needs to be addressed.
- Several times, there is an association of hopelessness with being pragmatic which must be addressed.
- Many people believe that only stupid people live in hope. This and any other such beliefs related to hopelessness should be addressed.
- Many people hold onto their fears related to hopelessness such as disappointment and disillusionment. These fears must be addressed before working on the actual hopelessness.
- Most people cope with hopelessness by inviting others to keep giving them hope and being with hopeful people. It is important to address these too.

It is helpful to consider these factors while designing statements.

Finally, the emotion of hopelessness can be addressed at both general and specific levels.

Addressing Hopelessness

If hopelessness is acute in nature, begin with step 9 and come back to steps 1–8 later.

1) Address the subconscious preprogramming of guilt of making others hopeless in the past. Repeat the first set of Redikall Reorganization statements (refer to Appendix III) by replacing ***** with "my guilt of making others feel hopeless in the past".
2) Address the association of hopelessness. Replace ***** in the statements with "my association of hopelessness with pragmatism" or any other similar feelings and associations.

3) Address the belief related to hopelessness. Replace ***** in the statements with "my belief that only stupid people live in hope" or similar feelings that need to be addressed.
4) Address the fears related to hopelessness. Replace ***** in the statements with "my fear of disappointment", "my fear of disillusionment", or similar fears that need to be addressed.
5) Address coping mechanisms of hopelessness. Replace ***** in the statements with "my need to cope with hopelessness by inviting others to keep giving me hope", "my need to cope with hopelessness by being with hopeful people".
6) Now address the general or specific aspects of hopelessness. Think about, recall, or imagine people, situations, events, and experiences that make you feel hopeless right now or have made you feel hopeless in the past. Assess the extent of the feeling within you on a scale of zero to ten (where zero means you have absolutely no hopelessness within, and ten means you have extremely high hopelessness within).
7) Repeat both sets of Redikall Reorganization statements by replacing ***** with "my hopelessness". You may make it specific if necessary. Replace ***** with, say, "my hopelessness at never finding love" or "my hopelessness at becoming a writer".
8) Reassess the feeling again on a scale of zero to ten as before. If the rating is still more than zero, repeat the statements. Be open and aware of the next layer of emotions and recite accordingly. Replace ***** with, say, "my hopelessness at never finding love", "my hurt at never finding love", or "my sadness at never finding love".
9) It is important to address the somatic—or bodily—sensations associated with the emotion of hopelessness too. You may ask yourself, "Where do I feel this hopelessness in my body right now?" You may feel, say, any ache or pain, discomfort, heaviness, numbness, stiffness, vibration, sensation, growling, pinching, weight, tingling, or itchiness in your body.
10) Assess that sensation in your body on a scale of zero to ten (where zero means you have absolutely no sensation in the body, and ten means you have extreme sensation in the body). Repeat both sets of Redikall Reorganization statements by replacing ***** with

the respective sensations in the body as you experience. Be open and aware of the changing body sensations and recite accordingly.

For example: You sense hopelessness in your right wrist, in the form of sharp pain. Replace ***** with "the sharp pain in my right wrist". Then your body sensations related to hopelessness change and you start to feel pain in your right elbow. Replace ***** with "the pain in my right elbow" in the statements.

11) When working with body discomfort and sensations for addressing the emotions, you may also work with specific keywords associated with that body part. Refer to Appendix I, Keywords for Minor Chakras.

Redikall note: The 250+ minor chakras are explained in the Essential Redikall Insights Course.

It is a good idea to always repeat the statements a minimum of three times for each set of statements or until you feel no more pain or other sensations in the body and you feel at ease.

(6) Heal Sadness, Grief, and Effects of Loss and Separation

What are sadness, grief, loss, and separation?

Sadness is a "low" feeling that arises out of the feeling that something is missing in life or not feeling okay about something in life.

Grief is a severe form of sadness that arises out of a loss of something or someone very dear to you.

The effects of loss and separation generate various kinds of feelings, the commonest being sadness and grief; however, sometimes people react with anger, rage, frustration, or helplessness.

The Redikall Foundation Technique gives you an amazing way to address various kinds of emotions generated out of feelings of loss and separation you feel because of a loved one's death.

Causative Factors

- Loss of people, pets, property, or possessions that are held dear
- Loss of health, loss of pain-free state of existence
- Loss of command over the circumstances
- Loss of emotional and loving connectivity
- Loss of prestige
- Loss of possibility of dream or project completion
- Loss of connectivity to the divine

The Evolutionary Response towards Sadness, Grief, Loss, and Separation

- Having suicidal tendencies
- Feeling sorrow, sadness, self-pity
- Feeling possessive and insecure towards what is left behind
- Feeling resentment and hatred, and grieving silently or overtly with crying and wailing
- Being unable to communicate, or at times, engaging in persistent conversation about the loss
- Working to a point of exhaustion and obsession to escape and suppress recognition of grief
- Searching for the divine, needing salvation, needing divine answers and solutions—searching for the deeper meaning of life

Important Factors about Sadness and Grief

There are many important aspects that are causative factors to sadness and grief. People hold onto them and often find it difficult to address them.

- There is a subconscious preprogramming of guilt because you didn't value what you had, the guilt of making others go through

sadness, grief, loss and separation. Therefore, this is the first aspect that needs to be addressed.
- Mostly, there is an association of sadness and grief with getting attention, concession, and care from loved ones.
- Many people think that sadness brings you closer to God, happy people are targeted, happiness is short lived, sadness and grief are the truth of life, or they cannot be happy if others around them are not happy. It is, therefore, important to address these beliefs.
- Many people hold onto their sadness and grief because they fear taking charge of their lives or fear they will be targeted for being happy. This fear must be addressed before working on the actual sadness and grief.

It is helpful to consider these factors while designing statements.

Finally, the emotion of sadness and grief can be addressed at a both general and specific levels.

Coping with Loss

Everything is transient in this universe. Life is a series of experiences, inputs, and outputs. However, we have a tendency to become attached to people, places, possibilities, and positions.

When you lose without your consent, at times, all of a sudden, you do take time to adjust to that loss. That adjustment begins at several levels.

- Adjustment at a physical level can lead you to cope with the physical absence; for example, using public transport after losing your vehicle.
- Adjustment at an emotional level is about coping with the emotional response to loss that can vary from grief, sadness, anger, and rage.
- Loss drives you to take charge of life, situations, and loved ones by opening up, choosing not to become victimized, and choosing not to feel helpless.

- An experience of loss makes it essential to forgive oneself, others, and God for the loss.
- A critical step to coping with loss is the acceptance of the post-loss scenario.
- It is important to discover the brilliance in the experience of loss and to effectively align to that brilliance.
- Finally, an experience of loss in the physical world can result in the understanding of the concept of co-creation through your higher consciousness.

Addressing Sadness, Grief, and the Effects of Loss and Separation

In the instance of an acute episode of sadness and grief, begin with step 9 and come back to the other steps later.

1) Address the subconscious preprogramming. This could be the guilt of not valuing what you had, the guilt of making others go through sadness, grief, or loss and separation. Repeat the first set of Redikall Reorganization Statements (refer to Appendix III) by replacing ***** with "my guilt of not valuing what I had", "my guilt of making others go through sadness, grief, loss, separation", or similar feelings which need to be addressed.

2) Address the association of sadness and grief. Replace ***** in the statements with "my association of sadness/grief with getting attention/concession" or "my association of sadness/grief with getting care from loved ones".

3) Address the belief related to sadness and grief. Replace ***** in the statements with "my belief that sadness brings me closer to God", "my belief that happy people are targeted", "my belief that happiness is short lived", "my belief that sadness and grief is the truth of life", "my belief that I cannot be happy if others around me are not happy", or similar set of beliefs which may need to be addressed.

4) Address the fears related to sadness and grief. Replace ***** in the statements with "my fear of taking charge of life", "my fear of

being targeted for being happy", or similar concerns which need to be addressed.

5) Address coping with the loss at a physical level. Replace ***** in the statements with "my loss of ……". Fill in the blank with whatever you have lost; for example, a person or a material thing.

6) Address coping with the loss at an emotional level. Replace ***** in the statements with "my …… due to the loss of my ……" Fill in the blanks with the emotion you feel and whatever you have lost; for example, feeling angry at losing your pet dog.

7) Address coping with the loss by taking charge of life, situations, and loved ones and not choosing to become victimized and helpless. Replace ***** in the statements with "my helpless and victimized feeling", "myself taking charge of life".

8) Address coping with loss through forgiveness of self, others, and God. Replace ***** in the statements with "the need to forgive ……". Fill in the blank with whomever you need to forgive.

9) Address coping with loss through acceptance of the post-loss scenario. Replace ***** in the statements with "my not okay feeling about ……" Fill in the blank with whatever scenario you are not okay with.

10) Address coping with loss by discovering the brilliance in the experience of loss and effective alignment to that brilliance. Replace ***** in the statements with "the brilliance in the experience of loss of ……" Fill in the blank with what you have lost.

11) Address coping with loss by conceiving through higher consciousness the concept of co-creation, resulting in an experience of "loss" in the physical world. Replace ***** in the statements with "my ownership and co-creation of loss".

12) Now address the general or specific sadness, grief, or loss and separation. Think about, recall, or imagine people, situations, events, and experiences that make you feel like this right now or have made you feel like this in the past. Assess how much of that feeling is within you on a scale of zero to ten (zero means you have absolutely no such emotion, and ten means you have extremely high emotion).

13) Repeat both sets of Redikall Reorganization statements by replacing ***** with "my sadness", "my grief", "my loss or separation". You may make it specific if necessary. Replace ***** with, say, "my sadness of losing my job" or "my grief of losing my mother".

14) Reassess the feeling again on a scale of zero to ten as before. If the rating is still more than zero, repeat the statements.

15) It is important to address the somatic—or bodily—sensations associated with these emotions of sadness, grief loss and, separation. You may ask yourself, "Where do I feel this emotion in my body right now?" You may feel, say, any ache or pain, discomfort, heaviness, numbness, stiffness, vibration, sensation, growling, pinching, weight, tingling, or itchiness in your body.

16) Assess that sensation in your body on a scale of zero to ten (zero means you have absolutely no sensation in the body, and ten means you have extreme sensation in the body). Repeat both sets of Redikall Reorganization statements by replacing ***** with the respective sensations in the body as you experience. Be open and aware of the changing sensations in your body and recite accordingly.

For example, you sense sadness in your throat in the form of a lump. Simply replace ***** with "the lump in my throat" in the statements. After you recite for a lump in the throat, your sensations change, and you start to feel burning in your throat. Replace ***** with "the burning in my throat" in the statements.

17) When working with body discomfort and sensations for addressing the emotions, you may also work with specific keywords associated with that body part. Refer to Appendix I, Keywords for Minor Chakras.

Redikall note: The 250+ minor chakras are explained in the Essential Redikall Insights Course.

It is a good idea to always repeat the statements a minimum of three times for each set of statements or until you feel no more pain or sensation in the body and you feel at ease.

(7) Resolve Confusion, Conflict, and Indecisiveness

What are confusion, conflict, and indecisiveness?

These three attributes go hand in hand.

Confusion is the inability to choose between various options and possibilities.

Conflict is the inability to opt between two options with opposite polarities. It can be a defense mechanism that arises out of fear of having clarity.

Indecisiveness is nonacceptance of the possible course of action due to various reasons, fears, and concerns.

Confusion and conflict are best treated at the somatic level—the level of the body, distinct from the mind.

If you were capable of gaining clarity, you would have gained it by now through your logical and linear thinking. The brilliant answers in life are always present and accessible through your subconscious mind. When you are upset about not being clear in your life, your filter mind gets congested further, and this makes it difficult to retrieve clarity and guidance from or through the subconscious mind. Hence, the focus should be on calming down.

Important Factors about Confusion, Conflict, and Indecisiveness

There are many important factors acting in the background making it difficult to address the feelings of confusion, conflict, and indecisiveness.

- There is a possibility of the subconscious preprogramming of feeling guilty for confusing others. Therefore, this is the first aspect that needs to be addressed.
- Most often, there is an unhealthy association of confusion with growth which must be addressed.
- Many people have a subconscious fear of gaining clarity and resistance towards clarity. This resistance and fear must be addressed before work can be done on the actual confusion, conflict, and indecisiveness.
- Eventually, people are likely to get clarity; however, they may have an emotional charge to the possible course of action which needs to be addressed through follow-ups to gain clarity, integrity, and confidence.

It is helpful to consider these factors while designing statements.

Finally, the emotions of confusion, conflict, and indecisiveness can be addressed at both general and specific levels.

Causative Factors of Confusion, Conflict, and Indecisiveness

- Various options threatening an unpleasant shift in the ground reality
- A possibility of pain after taking certain decisions
- A possibility of unknown factors
- A possibility of rejection by loved ones
- A possibility of loss of honor
- A possibility of deviation from morals, values, promises, past ancestral ambitions, dreams, ideas, and vision
- A possibility of disconnection with the divine or prime resource energy

Evolutionary Response to Confusion, Conflict, and Indecisiveness

- Remaining totally grounded, rational, and pragmatic in approach or becoming completely ungrounded and being out of touch with body consciousness

- Escaping through pleasure trips and overindulgence
- Showing rigidity and reluctance to flow
- Walling up and remaining emotionally unavailable
- Portraying of lack of confidence
- Being lethargic and sluggish in approach
- Lacking faith

Addressing Confusion, Conflict, and Indecisiveness

1) Address the subconscious preprogramming of feeling regret or guilt for confusing others. Repeat the first set of Redikall Reorganization Statements (refer to Appendix III) by replacing ***** with "the guilt of confusing others". Also, address the regret for judging others for being confused.

2) Address the association of confusion with growth. Repeat the statements by replacing ***** with "my association of confusion with growth". (At times people go through a leap of growth after a phase of conflict, confusion, or indecisiveness.)

3) Address the fear of gaining clarity. Repeat the statements by replacing ***** with "my fear of gaining clarity" or any other similar feelings which need to be addressed. Also, address the fear of acting or moving on after getting clarity.

4) Address the emotional charge related to the possible course of action. Repeat the statements by replacing ***** with "my emotional charge related to course of action" or any other similar feelings which need to be addressed.

5) Now address the general or specific confusion, conflict, and indecisiveness. Think about, recall, or imagine people, situations, events, and experiences that make you feel that way right now or have made you feel that way in the past. Assess the extent of feeling within you on a scale of zero to ten (zero means you have total clarity, feel decisive, and feel no emotional discomfort, and ten means you feel extremely confused, conflicted, or indecisive and experience extreme emotional discomfort).

6) Repeat both sets of Redikall Reorganization Statements by replacing ***** with "my confusion", "my conflict", or "my

indecisiveness". You may make it specific, if necessary. Replace ***** with, say, "my confusion deciding between career options", "my conflict with my boss", or "my indecisiveness of choosing between two job offers".

7) Reassess the feeling again on a scale of zero to ten as before. If the rating is still more than zero, repeat the statements. Be open and aware of the next layer of emotions and recite accordingly. Replace ***** with, say, "my sadness at not being able to decide between career options", "my anger at my boss".

8) It is important to address the somatic—or bodily—sensations associated with the emotions of confusion, conflict, and indecisiveness. You may ask yourself, "What situations, events and experiences make me feel confused, conflicted and indecisive? Where do I feel this emotion in my body right now?" You may feel, say, any ache or pain, discomfort, heaviness, numbness, stiffness, vibration, sensation, growling, pinching, weight, tingling, or itchiness in your body.

9) Assess those sensations in your body on a scale of zero to ten (zero means you have total clarity, feel decisive, and feel no physical discomfort, and ten means you feel extremely confused, conflicted, indecisive, or experience extreme physical discomfort).

10) Repeat both sets of Redikall Reorganization Statements by replacing ***** with the respective sensations in the body as you experience. Be open and aware of the changing body sensations and recite accordingly. For example, you sense confusion in your right temple, in the form of a throbbing pain. Replace ***** with "the throbbing pain in my right temple". If your body sensations for confusion change and you start feeling heaviness in your head, replace ***** with "heaviness in my head" in the statements.

When working with body discomfort and sensations for addressing the emotions, you may also work with specific keywords associated with that body part. Refer Appendix I, Keywords of Minor Chakras.

It is a good idea to always repeat the statements a minimum of three times for each set of statements or until you feel no more pain or sensation in the body and you feel at ease.

Redikall Note: Most of us at subconscious level have enough clarity. However, what is likely to happen after being clear or making up your mind may not be appealing or unknown to the conscious mind. For this reason, the resistance may appear in the form of confusion. Follow the symptomatic approach until you or the person you are helping calms down and clarity prevails. If necessary, follow the above-mentioned steps again.

(8) Heal Guilt and Shame

What are guilt and shame?

An unpleasant event that causes you to feel "not okay" about yourself could give rise to various feelings and emotions. Guilt, shame, low self-esteem, and low self-confidence are among them.

Guilt can be obvious when you have done something that you think is "not okay" morally. You could also feel guilty for unknown reasons. This happens when, at a subconscious level, you know that you are not in alignment with your soul plan.

Several types of suffering are directly or indirectly the result of guilt at the conscious or subconscious level.

Often, difficulties in life are the result of the need to punish yourself for something that has caused trivial or major guilt. It is possible to lead a guilt-free life, and you deserve to lead a guilt-free life. Interestingly, when you feel guilty, you directly or indirectly believe that you have erred (or made a mistake). This runs the risk of repeating these errors. On the contrary, reviving, recognizing, realigning, reorienting, and repositioning guilt helps you to clear your filter mind, reorganize folders in your subconscious mind, and realign to your unique GPS to get the right guidance for your decisions, actions, and implementations.

A guilt-free life makes you feel "okay" about yourself, enhances your self-esteem and self-confidence, and enables you to deservingly open up to receive the best in your life.

Shame can be a mild or a severe emotional discomfort originating from having done or having not done certain things, the result of which is dishonor to yourself or others around you.

Shame often helps people turn inwards and discover "self".

There are various kinds of shame. It can result from something as trivial as an unaware exposure of private body parts in public. More serious kinds of shame, including public humiliation, may result from failure in sports, academics, or business.

Few people can rise above serious humiliation. Most feel terribly "not okay" and succumb to self-reproach, self-condemnation, and self-introspection. Some may even withdraw from the public, forcefully isolating themselves, indulging in fantasies, and looking for spiritual solace and comfort. In severe cases, people may need to wander into consciousness in the metaphysical realm and befriend metaphysical elements, as they are least likely to be judgemental. Eventually, some people cannot distinguish between the physical and metaphysical worlds.

In the worst-case scenario, there is a constant need to remain connected to the metaphysical world and lose touch with the physical reality and the distinction between the two. This happens in cases of schizophrenia.

Because shame also helps people in spiritual growth, there can be a reluctance to treat shame or recover from it because eliminating it could block further spiritual growth. A person who has gone through shame and embarrassment may go through a kind of recursive loop by seeking help from someone else because they feel ashamed speaking about the past experience.

A major reason for resistance when addressing shame is the fear of inviting shameful situations once again.

While addressing shame, it is important to be non-judgemental, noncritical, and compassionate. Address the resistance and associated fears to let go of the feeling of shame before you address the shame. It is very important to restore the honor that you deserve.

Shame can be healed in the same way that guilt can be healed.

Important Factors about Guilt and Shame

There are many important aspects that generate guilt and shame. These make people hold onto them, which makes them challenging to address.

- There is a subconscious preprogramming of making others feel guilty or putting others to shame that does not allow us to address the guilt and shame within. Therefore, this is the first aspect that needs to be addressed.
- Frequently, experiences of guilt and shame have helped an individual to grow well in life. In such a case, the association of guilt and shame with growth must be worked with.
- Many people think that guilt as a virtue or shame has helped them to see spiritual growth, and there is a reluctance to recover from it. It is, therefore, important to address this belief.
- Many people hold on to their guilt to remind them not to make the same mistakes again. There is a resistance and fear of letting go of shame because of fear of inviting shameful situations again. This resistance and fear must be addressed before working on the actual guilt and shame.

It is helpful to consider these factors while designing statements.

Finally, the emotion of guilt and shame can be addressed at both general and specific levels.

Causative Factors for Guilt, Regret, and Shame

- While survivor's guilt is rare in life, it can be very severe. It is guilt over surviving alone while many people you knew died in a natural

disaster or accidents. Occasionally, this could be the result of past-life preprogramming of the survivor's guilt
- Emotional hurt and pain to self or others
- Loss of control
- Rejection
- Public showdown or social embarrassment
- Lack of success
- Distanced from the divine, guru figures, religion

Evolutionary Pattern of Guilt, Regret, and Shame

- Experiencing suicidal tendencies
- Having desire for self-punishment
- Exhibiting obsessive and over-cautious behavior
- Feeling self-hatred
- Feeling low self-esteem
- Being reluctant to succeed
- Feeling distanced from anything spiritual

Addressing Guilt and Shame

1) The first step is to address the subconscious preprogramming of making others regret, feel guilty or putting others to shame. Repeat the first set of Redikall Reorganization statements (refer to Appendix III) by replacing ***** in the statements with "the guilt of making others feel guilty", "the shame of putting others to shame", or similar feelings which need to be addressed.

2) Address the association of regret, guilt and shame. Replace ***** in the statements with "my association of guilt/shame/regret with growth" or "my belief that guilt/shame/regret make me grow in life".

3) Address the belief related to regret, guilt and shame. Replace ***** in the statements with "my belief that guilt is a virtue" or "my belief that experiences of shame/regret have given me spiritual growth".

4) Address the fear associated with regret, guilt and shame. Replace ***** in the statements with "my fear of letting go of guilt and shame", "my fear of making mistakes again", "my fear of inviting shameful situations again", or similar feelings which need to be addressed.

5) Now address the general or specific guilt and shame. Think about, recall, or imagine people, situations, events, and experiences that make you feel guilty or ashamed right now or have made you feel guilty or ashamed in the past. Assess the level right now within you on a scale of zero to ten (zero means you have absolutely no guilt or shame, and ten means you have extremely high guilt/shame).

6) Repeat both sets of Redikall Reorganization statements by replacing ***** with "my guilt" or "my shame/regret". You may make it specific, if necessary. Replace ***** with, say, "my guilt for not being a good mother" or "my shame for calling my teacher mommy when I was four years old".

7) Reassess the feeling again on a scale of zero to ten as before. If the rating is still more than zero, repeat the statements. Also, as you recite, allow your emotions to come to your awareness, layer by layer, and continue to recite them. After reciting for guilt, if you realize you feel angry at yourself for what happened, repeat the statements this time for this next layer of emotion. Replace ***** with "my anger at myself".

8) It is important to address the somatic—or bodily—sensations associated with feelings of guilt and shame. You may ask yourself, "Where do I feel this emotion in my body right now?" You may feel, say, any ache or pain, discomfort, heaviness, numbness, stiffness, vibration, sensation, growling, pinching, weight, tingling, or itchiness in your body. Assess that sensation in the body on a scale of zero to ten (zero means you have absolutely no sensation in the body, and ten means you have extreme sensation in the body). Repeat both sets of Redikall Reorganization statements, replacing ***** with the respective sensations in the body that you experience. For example, you sense guilt in your middle back in the form of a weight. Simply replace ***** with "the weight on my

back" in the statements. Or if you sense shame causing stiffness in your back, simply replace ***** with "this stiffness in my back" in the statements.

9) Reassess the sensation in the body again on a scale of zero to ten as before. If the rating is still more than zero, recite again. Be open and aware of the changing sensations in your body and recite accordingly. For example, after you recite for weight on the back, your sensations change, and you start feeling heavy in your chest. Replace ***** with "the heaviness in my chest" in the statements.

10) When working with body discomfort and sensations for addressing the emotions, you may also work with specific keywords associated with that body part. Refer Appendix I, Keywords for Minor Chakras.

Redikall Note: The 250+ minor chakras are explained in the Essential Redikall Insights Course.

It is a good idea to always repeat the statements a minimum of three times for each set of statements or until you feel no more pain or sensation in your body and you feel at ease.

(9) Heal Low Self-Esteem and Low Self-Confidence

What are low self-esteem and low self-confidence?

Low self-esteem can be an acquired issue or can be a part of soul-level preprogramming.

Some people are born feeling low about themselves. This may happen with a child born as a fifth female child in rural India where the family was desperately looking forward to a male child. It may happen with a child born into a family that is socially condemned.

Some people's self-esteem and confidence can be the result of preprogramming after having harmed someone else's self-esteem or confidence. At the soul level, you may have chosen to experience what it is like to feel "not okay" about yourself.

There are several contributing factors that add to low self-esteem. These can range from poor academic achievement to major setbacks in life.

Most people who suffer from low self-esteem may regress to reveal a preprogramming from a lifetime in which they were arrogant and harmed others. Low self-esteem, perhaps, is a soul-level need for assurance that you remain humble.

Some super achievers battle their low self-esteem by setting big challenges. However, their achievement when they overcome their challenge is not always adequate compensation and does not assure positive self-esteem. This is because, no matter how much they achieve, there are still unmet goals and objectives based on higher expectations generated by the level of achievement. You need to recognize the possibility of these patterns in your life and resolve to be "okay" about yourself. Gracious acceptance is the key.

Low self-esteem automatically causes loss of confidence. You can have low confidence caused by self-doubt and an inhibitory approach to yourself.

Many times, people do prefer to cling to low self-confidence out of their fear of being arrogant about their outstanding success. Low self-esteem often assures a pseudo sense of social security through leading a mediocre life, while the higher level of self-confidence and self-belief is often falsely associated with loneliness.

Important Factors about Low Self-Esteem and Low Self-Confidence

There are many important factors that cause low self-esteem and low self-confidence. You must explore and address them, layer by layer, and heal the past where your self-esteem and confidence level dipped.

- There is a subconscious preprogramming of harming someone else's self-esteem and confidence. You feel guilty about this. Therefore, this is the first aspect that needs to be addressed.

- Usually there is an unhealthy and incorrect association of self-esteem with achievement and confidence with arrogance. It is important to address such erroneous associations.
- Many people think that having high self-esteem and confidence makes them arrogant and can harm others. It is, therefore, important to address this belief.

It is helpful to consider these factors while designing your statements.

It is always a good idea to identify and address what you don't feel okay with.

Causative Factors for Low Self-Esteem and Low Self-Confidence

- Inadequate material resources
- Lack of sex appeal and attractive appearance
- Lack of power
- Repeated rejection
- Feeling not good enough
- Lack of success or delayed success
- Perceived distance from the divine

Evolutionary response

- Lacking the desire to live or survive
- Lacking interest in pleasurable activities in life
- Playing a victim or the "poor me" game
- Inviting repeated rejection
- Inviting criticism and blame
- Living in self-doubt
- Feeling of unworthiness of divine grace

Addressing Low Self-Esteem and Low Self-Confidence

1) Address the subconscious preprogramming of harming someone else's self-esteem and confidence and thereby feeling guilty about it. Repeat the first set of Redikall Reorganization statements (refer

to Appendix III) by replacing ***** with "my guilt of harming others' self-esteem and confidence" or any other similar feelings which need to be addressed.

2) Address the association of self-esteem with achievement. Repeat the statements by replacing ***** with "my association of self-esteem with achievement".

3) Address the belief that high self-esteem and confidence would make you arrogant and cause you to harm others. Repeat the statements by replacing ***** with "my belief that my high self-esteem and confidence would make me arrogant and harm others".

4) Now address the feeling of not being okay about yourself. Also, be aware of the somatic—or bodily—sensations that you experience when you do not feel okay about self. For example, when you do not feel okay about yourself, you may experience ache or pain, discomfort, heaviness, stiffness, vibration, or numbness.

5) Ask yourself, "What people, situations, events, and experiences make me feel 'not okay' about myself? How does it feel in my body when I am not okay about myself?"

6) Assess your response on a scale of zero to ten (zero means you feel completely okay about yourself and feel no body sensations or discomfort, and ten means you feel extremely not okay about yourself and experience extreme body sensations and discomfort).

7) Repeat both sets of Redikall Reorganization statements by replacing ***** with "my feeling of not okay with self", "my feeling of not okay with self when I speak publicly", "this choking in my throat when I am not okay with myself", or "my shaking legs when I have to confront someone".

8) Reassess the sensations in your body again on a scale of zero to ten as before. If the rating is still more than zero, recite again. Be open and aware of the changing sensations in your body and recite accordingly.

9) When working with body discomfort and sensations for addressing the emotions, you may also work with specific keywords associated with that body part. Refer the Appendix I, Keywords for Minor Chakras.

Redikall note: The 250+ minor chakras are explained in the Essential Redikall Insights Course.

It is a good idea to always repeat the statements a minimum of three times for each set of statements or until you feel no more pain or sensation in the body and you feel at ease.

(10) Heal Relationships

The dynamics of relationships are shaped by the need for certain human-level and soul-level experiences of people involved in relationships. As your needs shift, the relationship dynamics shift as well. Most of the time it is common to expect others to shift in order to bring about a positive shift in the relationship. This brings in a deadlock in the dynamics.

Here you need to note that people with a complementary need for experiences remain in the relationship for a long period of time, provided they do not expect the other person to be like them. For example, an introvert individual would share a long-lasting relationship with an extrovert individual, or a logical and analytical individual would share a long-lasting companionship with a free-flowing and at times impulsive personality.

Aware acceptance with love can restore the health of any relationship. People and your relationship with them is not our problem. How you perceive people, how you project your inconsistency through people, and how you respond to people are essentially major problems in relationships.

Perception of people is often influenced by socio-economic, educational, and religious conditioning. For example, a conservative farmer may condemn the career-minded approach of a married woman, while a city dweller may respectfully encourage the career-oriented approach of a married woman.

So, in order to develop healthy relationships, turn inward and check how you perceive:

- Yourself in the relationship
- Other(s) in the relationship
- The dynamics of the relationship

There are seven types of relationships based on individual and spiritual growth:

I. **Relationships based on material needs.** In these relationships, people may share a common ground, property, and finances. The material-level sharing sustains these relationships and also creates conflicts and problems in the relationships. The healing begins when the elements of joy and pleasure are added.

II. **Relationships based on pleasure, enjoyment, and sex.** People remain in these relationships for common pleasurable interests. For example, sharing a hobby, joyous activities, or a conjugal relationship. These relationships at times suffer due to emotional pain, and the relationship health is restored when the focus returns to sharing the moments of mutual joy and pleasure rather than focusing on past hurts and pain. The healing begins when expectations are set realistically and commitments are based on expectations.

III. **Relationships based on sharing a common system.** These may be based, for example, on an organizational structure, a social structure and system, or a political system. These relationships often suffer due to power games as well as the violation and intrusion of boundaries. The health in the relationship restores when individual positions and hierarchy are honored and abided by everyone in the relationship. Also, operating from love and forgiveness over and above the mutual respect is important.

IV. **Relationships based on love, acceptance, and unconditionality.** Examples of this sort of relationship are relationships between grandparents and grandchildren, and relationships between pet owners and their pets. These relationships may suffer when conditionality is demanded. The healing begins when the communication is enhanced and feelings are allowed to be expressed and respected.

V. **Relationships based on mutual respect and honor.** These relationships can exist between professional colleagues, social acquaintances, or members of a sports team. These relationships sometimes suffer because of judgment, criticism, humiliation, and dishonor. The restoration can happen if the focus remains on common objectives and goals.

VI. **Relationships based on common objectives, goals, visions, and missions.** Examples are relationships among people working on a research project, relationships among trustees of a committed organization. These relationships may suffer due to distraction, disputes, and differences of interest. Relationships can be restored if the focus remains on the larger picture.

VII. **Relationships based on experiencing oneness.** Though very few relationships reach this level, people discover themselves through others and discover others through themselves. They understand that those in the relationship are essentially their extension and their projection. These kinds of relationships are possible when individuals in the relationship are complete within themselves, totally aligned to their life plans, completely oriented to the highest objective in their life plans, and have taken correct position in their lives, which reflects in appropriateness of the position taken by all around them. However, they need to ensure that they remain grounded well.

While healing relationships, keep the following pointers in mind:

- Others are not really your problems; your problems are derived from your perceptions based on your preprogramming and your responses.
- Avoid waiting for others to change. Instead, look at the possibility of changing your perceptions and responses.

- Do not succumb to identifying others' incorrectness and your own correctness. Most people think they are right in their responses irrespective of others' perceptions.
- The blame game in relationships is counterproductive.
- Presume that others in the relationship are not going to change or shift. Look at the easiest shift you can bring in your approach.
- While describing matters in a relationship, begin the sentence by saying "I recognize …". For example, "I recognize that my mother has been unfair to me" or "I recognize that my partner is cheating on me". Using the words *I recognize* brings about detached neutrality.
- Most relationship issues are caused by incorrect alignment, incorrect orientation, and incorrect position given to the relationship through the subconscious mind; for example, a woman expecting her husband to treat her the way her father did, or a person expecting a daughter or wife to fulfil the vacuum left behind by his late mother.
- Heal your experience in and through relationships to heal the relationship dynamics. For example, if you are in an abusive relationship, there could be a history of a past abuse of some kind. Or you may have a soul-level need to experience abuse for certain reasons. If you address your need to be abused, you will experience a positive shift in the relationship dynamics.

Addressing Relationships

Redikall note: It is advisable to heal one relationship at a time. Or you can heal the experience generated in the relationship (refer to the chapters that correspond to relevant emotions).

1) Address the perceptions that you carry about a person, object, or abstract concept in the relationship.

    a) For example, you perceive a particular relationship to be unhealthy for you. Refer to the first set of Redikall Reorganization statements (refer to Appendix III) by replacing

***** with "my unhealthy relationship". Or be specific and say "my unhealthy relationship with #####" (where ##### is the name of person, object, or abstract concept in the relationship).

b) Or you feel trapped in a relationship. Replace ***** in the statements with "my trapped feeling in the relationship". You may make it as specific as possible.

2) Think of a person, object, or abstract concept you are in relationship with. How does the relationship make you feel? Assess your emotional charge on a scale of zero to ten (zero means you have no emotional charge at all with respect to that relationship, and ten means you have extremely high emotional charge with respect to that relationship).

3) Repeat the first set of Redikall Reorganization statements (refer to Appendix III)) by replacing ***** with the name of the person, object, or abstract phenomenon or the emotion they trigger in you. For example, replace ***** in the statements with "my relationship with my mother", "my relationship with my husband", "my anger at my mother", or "my feeling of humiliation from my wife".

4) Reassess the feeling again on a scale of zero to ten as before. The following possibilities apply:

a) **Your emotional charge has become zero, and you feel totally fine with respect to that relationship.** In this case, you can choose to work with another emotion related to that person or object or another relationship in a similar manner, or you may simply celebrate your emotional-pain-free existence for that relationship.

b) **Your emotional charge is reduced, but is still more than zero, and you feel slightly better but not yet totally fine with respect to the relationship.** In this case, you can recite a few more times until you feel calm and at ease. Also, as you recite, allow your emotions to come to your awareness, layer by layer, and continue to recite about them for the next few days.

c) **Your emotional charge is better; however, another layer of emotion has come to your awareness with respect to that relationship.** You are advised to repeat the first set of statements where you replace ***** with the new emotion. For example, after anger at your mother, the next layer of emotion that surfaces is a feeling of helplessness. Replace ***** with "my feeling of helplessness towards my mother".

d) **Your emotional charge is same or has increased.** This suggests a subconscious resistance to address this relationship. You can use the second set of statements where you replace ***** with "my resistance to heal this relationship with ######" (where ###### stands for the person, object, or abstract concept in the relationship).

e) When you calm down and your mind and thoughts become still, and you are in the thoughtless state of mind, you will get the clear picture that will help you understand why things are the way they are and how you could modify your approach. Follow the guidance.

5) Reassess the level of emotional charge once more on a scale of zero to ten as before. Ensure that the charge is at level zero: you feel calm and at ease.

It is a good idea to always repeat the statements a minimum of three times for each set of statements or until you feel no more emotional charge and you feel at ease.

(11) Heal Professional Challenges

It is important to understand and address professional challenges. Keep in mind that *profession* can mean different things to different people.

- For people who are struggling with survival, profession is a means for survival in life.
- Some people use profession as a means to enjoy life. They seek to enjoy the profession or the money they earn through the profession. However, often the pain arising out of the profession needs to be addressed.
- Some people seek to use their professions for extra power. However, the power games they play eventually make them feel powerless, and they may need assistance.
- There are people who love being in a particular profession. However, occasionally they may generate hatred from the loved ones, fans, or people around them, and they may need assistance.
- Some people choose a particular profession for honor and yet, when they do not get the kind of honor they feel they deserve, they feel terrible and may need assistance.
- There are people who are in total alignment with their dreams, ideas, and visions with respect to their professions. At the other extreme, some people are not aligned with their professions, and their professions seem to be taking away from their dreams, ideas, and visions.
- Some people feel "at one" with their professions and can't imagine being in any other profession. At the other extreme, there are people who feel totally uncomfortable in the professions they have taken up, and they struggle to discover why they are doing what they are doing.

Your profession is a wonderful opportunity to grow in your personal and your spiritual life. Discomforts you feel from your profession indicate that it's time to evolve. Probably you are stagnating with the stand you have taken with respect to your profession.

Whatever profession you have chosen, in order to address your professional challenges, your objective should be to go to the next level. Here are some examples:

- If you have difficulty in survival through your profession, focus on discovering the joy and happiness you derive from your profession.

Let's say that you feel that your profession does not give you enough means for survival. Rather than fighting with survival, go one level higher and discover the joy in your profession. As you do that, the means for survival will be taken care of. For example, replace ***** in the first set of Redikall Reorganization statements with "the joy in my profession": "I revive the joy in my profession".

- If you have difficulty enjoying your profession, focus on being in alignment with the system offered by your profession and discovering your personal powers. If you are not enjoying your profession, how about trying to discover the flow and looking at the possibility of being in the flow (or flowing with the flow) within your profession; then you will start enjoying it. Replace ***** in the statements with "the flow within the system".
- If you have difficulty in accepting the system offered by your profession, focus on loving and embracing yourself as a part of the profession and loving and embracing the profession as a part of you. Simply focus on love for your profession and for yourself as a professional. Replace ***** in the statements with "the love for the system".
- If you have difficulty with hatred and rejection of your profession or the professional in you, discover the honor and respect through your profession and for the professional in you. In other words, you hate your profession or hate, perhaps, yourself as the professional. Simply honour and impart dignity and respect to yourself and your profession. Replace ***** in the statements with "the honor for my profession and the professional in me".
- If you have difficulty in respecting your profession and the professional in you, discover the alignment with the purpose of your life. Replace ***** in the statements with "being aligned to my life purpose".
- If you have difficulty in being aligned with the purpose of your life, then just *be* yourself.

Redikall note: The concept of the purpose of life is examined in full in the Advanced Redikall Consciousness Course.

Addressing the Perception of Negativities, Ghosts, Spirits, and Entities

Redikall note: It is advisable to heal the perception of one entity at a time. Alternatively, you can heal the experience generated by them. Address the perceptions that you carry about a person, object, or abstract concept in the relationship.

    a) For example, you perceive a particular person, experience, or an entity to be life threatening for you. Recite first set of Redikall Reorganization statements (refer to Appendix III) by replacing ***** with "my perception of the threat to my life" or be specific: "my perception of threat to my life because of #####" (where ##### is the name of person, object, or abstract concept in the relationship).

    b) Or, if you feel restricted because of these negativities, ghosts, or entities, replace ***** in the statements with "my feeling of being restricted by ####". #### represents a particular entity that makes you feel restricted. You may make it as specific as possible.

6) Think of the ghost, negativity, entity, or spirit and imagine it to be in front of you. Repeat the first set of Redikall Reorganization statements by replacing ***** with the person, situation, ghost, or abstract phenomenon or the emotion they trigger in you. For example, replace ***** in the statements with "ghost in my room" or "negativity in my family members".

7) Think of the ghost, negativity, entity, or spirit. How does that make you feel? Assess your emotional charge on a scale of zero to ten (zero means you have no emotional charge at all with respect to that relationship, and ten means you have extremely high emotional charge with respect to that relationship).

8) Reassess the feeling again on a scale of zero to ten as before. The following possibilities apply:

a) **Your emotional charge has become zero.** You feel totally fine with respect to that entity. In that case, you can choose to work with another emotion related to that person, situation, ghost, or abstract phenomenon or another entity in a similar manner or simply celebrate your emotional pain-free existence for that entity.

b) **Your emotional charge is reduced, but it is still more than zero.** You feel slightly better but not yet totally fine with respect to that entity, situation, ghost, or abstract phenomenon. In this case, you can recite a few more times till you feel calm and at ease. Also, as you recite, allow your emotions to come to your awareness, layer by layer, and continue to recite on them for the next few days.

c) **Your emotional charge is better; however, another layer of emotion has come to your awareness with respect to that entity, situation, ghost, or abstract phenomenon.** You are advised to repeat the first set of statements, replacing ***** with the new entity, situation, ghost, or abstract phenomenon. For example, after addressing "ghost in my room", the next layer of emotion that surfaces is a feeling of helplessness. Replace ***** with "my feeling of helplessness towards my mother".

d) **Your emotional charge is same or has increased.** This suggests a subconscious resistance to address this relationship. You can use the second set of statements, replacing ***** with "my resistance to heal this relationship with ######" (###### stands for the person, object, or abstract concept in the relationship).

When you calm down and your mind and thoughts become still, in the thoughtless state of mind, you will get the clear picture which will help you understand why things are the way they are and how you could modify your approach. Follow the guidance.

9) Reassess the level of emotional charge once more on a scale of zero to ten as before. Ensure that the charge is at level zero (you feel calm and at ease).

10) It is a good idea to always repeat the statements a minimum of three times for each set of statements or until you feel no more emotional charge and you feel at ease.

Appendix I: Keywords of Minor Chakras

Foundation keywords are associated with major or minor energy centers in your body, known as chakras. These are exclusively chakra-based guidance phrases. The body intelligence often gives you a clue to address certain beliefs. While doing a healing consultation or while reciting the Redikall Reorganization statements (RRS), if the pain or discomfort suddenly shifts to a distant part of the body, know that the body consciousness is drawing your attention to address the next layer of associated belief, thought, or emotion. You may have to work through several layers before you eventually connect to the core of your issue. That is when you feel peaceful, practically pain free, and blissful as you can see through your entire issue or challenge with an enhanced awareness gained by your Redikall Crystalline Mind.

For example, while addressing headache, if the pain shifts to the right shoulder (CR1, right relief chakra, need for freedom from the past), now you need to address certain future concerns. As you address the future concern through the RRS, the pain may shift to right temple (FR7, right clarity chakra, confusion, conflict, and indecisiveness), which indicates a state of confusion. As you address the confusion through the RRS, the pain can shift to ankle (TR1, right strength chakra, a sense of shortcomings and weakness), which indicates that body consciousness has drawn your attention to certain shortcomings or weaknesses. You do not necessarily have to remember all these chakras; they are listed in this appendix. Or you can access them on our website, www.redikallhealing.com

Take the following steps when the pain or discomfort in the body shifts:

1) Determine the affected body part.
2) Locate the affected chakras as shown in the picture.

3) Read the foundation keyword of the corresponding chakra.
4) Replace ***** with the Redikall foundation keywords and recite the affirmation until the pain subsides or shifts.
5) Repeat the process from the first step if the pain shifts.

You need to simply keep replacing ***** with the foundation keywords until you reach a calm state.

Redikall note: You will learn more on these keywords and their detailed explanation in subsequent courses of the Redikall Insights Curriculum.

(I) Face Minor Chakras

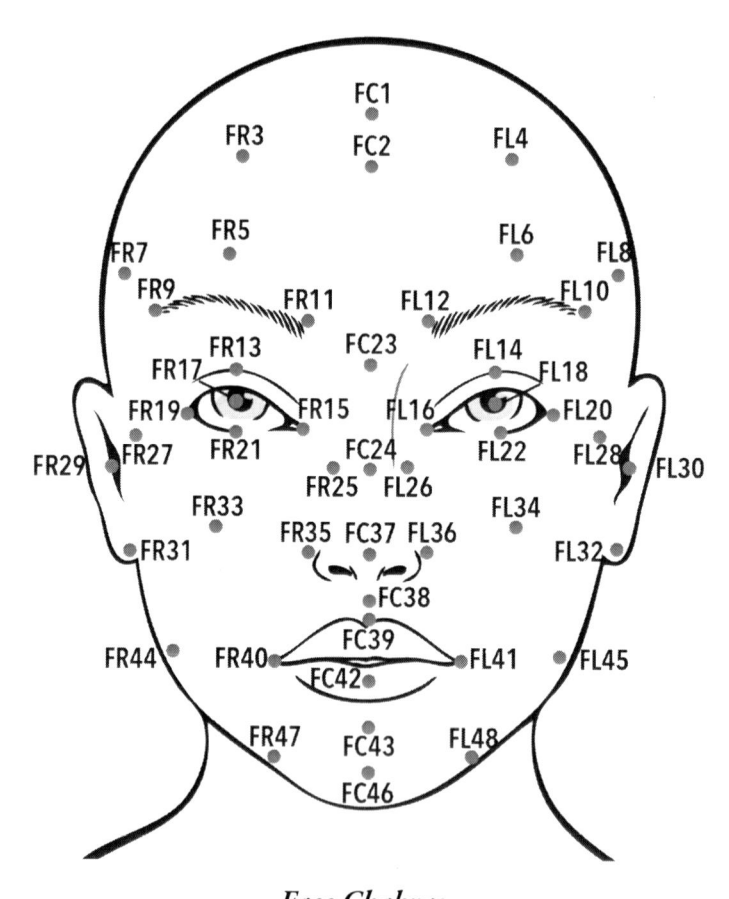

Face Chakras

(I) Face Minor Chakras

Chakra Code	Chakra Name	Position	Foundation Keyword
FC1	Faith chakra	Center point of top of the forehead (where women put the *sindoor*)	**Need for faith**
FC2	Promises chakra	Center of forehead one and a half fingers below the faith chakra	**Oaths, vows, and promises**
FR3	Right liberation chakra	Center point between the faith chakra and the clarity chakra (right side)	**Need to be liberated**
FL4	Left liberation chakra	Center point between the faith chakra and the clarity chakra (left side)	**Need to liberate**
FR5	Right approval chakra	One finger above the center of the eyebrow (right side)	**Feeling of being disliked and disapproved**
FL6	Left approval chakra	One finger above the center of the eyebrow (left side)	**Disapproval of #####**
FR7	Right clarity chakra	Temple (right side)	**Confusion, conflict, and indecisiveness**
FL8	Left clarity chakra	Temple (left side)	**Confusion and conflict in action plan**
FR9	Right awareness assimilation chakra	Outer end of the eyebrow (right side)	**Inability to apply what I learnt**

Chakra Code	Chakra Name	Position	Foundation Keyword
FL10	Left awareness assimilation chakra	Outer end of the eyebrow (left side)	Inability to apply the inner awareness and knowledge
FR11	Right assertion chakra	Beginning of the eyebrow near the bridge of the nose (right side)	Sensitivity to others' expression
FL12	Left assertion chakra	Beginning of the eyebrow near the bridge of the nose (left side)	Need for freedom to express, question or assert
FR13	Right neutral observation chakra	Upper eyelid (right side)	Need for neutral observation of the outer inconsistencies
FL14	Left neutral observation chakra	Upper eyelid (left side)	Need for neutral observation of the inner inconsistencies
FR15	Right integrity chakra	Inner angle, corner of the eye (right side)	Feeling of being betrayed, cheated or let down
FL16	Left integrity chakra	Inner angle, corner of the eye (left side)	Feeling of lacking integrity with self, higher self or others
FR17	Right neutral perception chakra	Eyeball (right side)	Need for correction in perception
FL18	Left neutral perception chakra	Eyeball (left side)	Image consciousness

Chakra Code	Chakra Name	Position	Foundation Keyword
FR19	Right neutral observation to inaccessible chakra	Outer angle, corner of the eye (right side)	Need for neutrality towards the peripheral inconsistencies
FL20	Left neutral observation to inaccessible chakra	Outer angle, corner of the eye (left side)	Need for neutrality towards the shadow self
FR21	Right catharsis chakra	Lower eyelid (right side)	Past grief due to outer circumstances
FL22	Left catharsis chakra	Lower eyelid (left side)	Internal grief due to inappropriate decision or action taken in the past
FC23	Cheerfulness chakra	Beginning of the nose	Need to remain cheerful irrespective of outer circumstances
FC24	Diplomacy chakra	Bridge of the nose (middle part)	Need for communicating with diplomacy
FR25	Right appreciation chakra	Side of the nose (right side)	Feeling of not being appreciated and being undervalued
FL26	Left appreciation chakra	Side of the nose (left side)	Need to appreciate and value self and others
FR27	Right proactive peace chakra	Temporomandibular joint (right side)	Suppressed rage against other's rage

Chakra Code	Chakra Name	Position	Foundation Keyword
FL28	Left proactive peace chakra	Temporomandibular joint (left side)	**Suppressed rage**
FR29	Right listening chakra	Ear (right side)	**Reluctance to listen to others**
FL30	Left listening chakra	Ear (left side)	**Reluctance to listen to inner voice**
FR31	Right confession chakra	Ear lobe (right side)	**Need to admit mistakes to others**
FL32	Left confession chakra	Ear lobe (left side)	**Need to admit mistakes to self**
FR33	Right amiability chakra	Cheek (right side)	**Need to be sensitive to others' irritation**
FL34	Left amiability chakra	Cheek (left side)	**Irritability**
FR35	Right resources chakra	Nostril (right side)	**Inhibitions in receiving resources**
FL36	Left resources chakra	Nostril (left side)	**Inhibition in channeling resources**
FC37	Popularity and recognition chakra	Tip of the nose	**Reluctance to be popular**
FC38	Consolidation of existence chakra	Groove between the nose and the upper lip	**Need to overcome the effect of devastation**
FC39	Earth bound existence acceptance chakra	Upper lip	**Need to accept the earthbound existence**

Chakra Code	Chakra Name	Position	Foundation Keyword
FR40	Right fairness chakra	Corner of the lip (right side)	Feeling of being abused or unfairly taken advantage of
FL41	Left fairness chakra	Corner of the lip (left side)	Suppressing the desire to abuse or being unfair to self or others
FC42	Confidentiality chakra	Lower lip	Need for confidentiality
FC43	Blessings chakra	Groove between the lower lip and the chin	Effect of the curses and adverse statements made by others
FR44	Right anger recognition chakra	Jaw angle (right side)	Reserved distress towards others' anger
FL45	Left anger recognition chakra	Jaw angle (left side)	Reserved anger at self or others
FC46	Wisdom chakra	Chin	Need for inner wisdom
FR47	Right gratitude for grounding chakra	Three fingers away from the chin on jaw line (right side)	Need to be grateful towards the external grounding factors
FL48	Left gratitude for grounding chakra	Three fingers away from the chin on jaw line (left side)	Need to be grateful towards the internal grounding factors

(II) Neck Minor Chakras

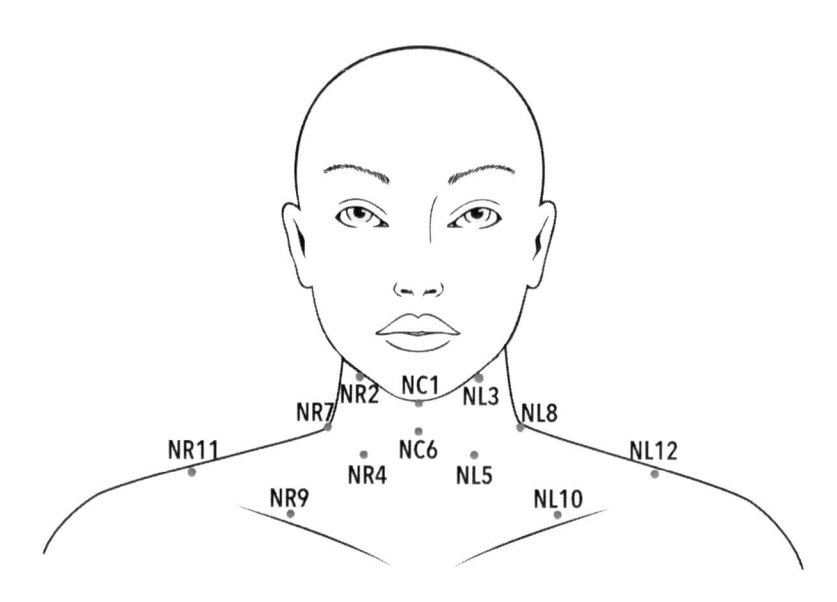

Neck Chakras

Chakra Code	Chakra Name	Position	Foundation Keyword
NC1	Effective proposition chakra	Under the chin (double chin area)	Need for an effective proposition
NR2	Right relaxation chakra	Below the wisdom tooth, soft part of the neck (right side)	Need to take the permission from others to relax
NL3	Left relaxation chakra	Below the wisdom tooth, soft part of the neck (left side)	Need to relax
NR4	Right articulation chakra	One finger to the right of the cricoid cartilage, or Adam's apple	Difficulty in understanding verbal communication from others

Chakra Code	Chakra Name	Position	Foundation Keyword
NL5	Left articulation chakra	One finger to the left of the cricoid cartilage, or Adam's apple	Difficulty in verbal expression
NC6	Option chakra	Three fingers away from the chin on the central neck line	Need to opt for the right choice
NR7	Right humility chakra	Angle between the neck and shoulder (right side)	Sensitivity to rudeness
NL8	Left humility chakra	Angle between the neck and shoulder (left side)	Need to remain humble
NR9	Right cherish chakra	Above the clavicle (right side)	Rejection from others
NL10	Left cherish chakra	Above the clavicle (left side)	Tendency to reject #####
NR11	Right ease chakra	Mid-shoulder (right side)	Burdened feeling
NL12	Left ease chakra	Mid-shoulder (left side)	Need to burden oneself or others

(III) Scalp Minor Chakras

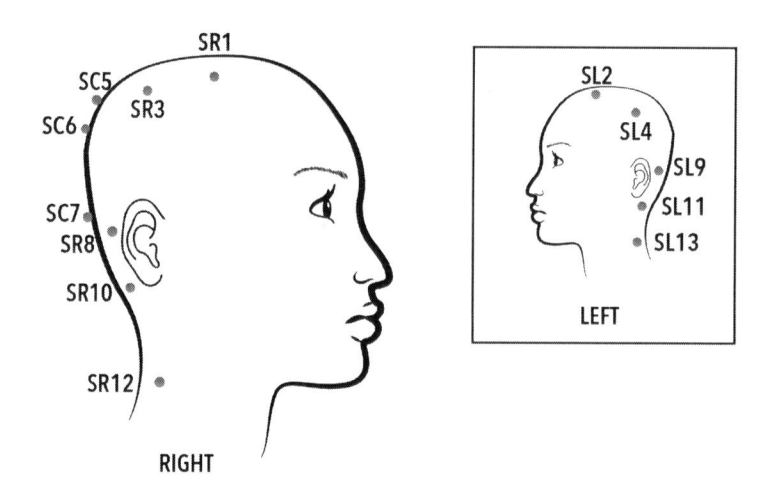

Scalp Chakras

Chakra Code	Chakra Name	Position	Foundation Keyword
SR1	Right commitment chakra	Lateral fontanelle (right side) (Three fingers to the right of the crown chakra, towards the right ear)	Feeling of being let down by others
SL2	Left commitment chakra	Lateral fontanelle (left side) (Three fingers to the left of the crown chakra, towards the left ear)	Feeling of letting down self or others
SR3	Right defense adaptation chakra	Parietal eminence (right side)	Reluctance to accept the change in the way people defend themselves

Chakra Code	Chakra Name	Position	Foundation Keyword
SL4	Left defense adaptation chakra	Parietal eminence (left side)	**Reluctance to accept the change in the way I defend myself**
SC5	Consciousness chakra	Between the right and left parietal eminence	**Need to enhance consciousness**
SC6	Divinity chakra	One and a half fingers above the third eye chakra	**Need to experience divinity**
SC7	Balance chakra	A notch below the occipital bone	**Anticipation of imbalance**
SR8	Right sincerity chakra	Behind the ear where the spectacles end (right side)	**Studious approach expected by others**
SL9	Left sincerity chakra	Behind the ear where the spectacles end (left side)	**Studious approach due to self-expectations**
SR10	Right roleplay acceptance chakra	Tiara point where the hair band or tiara ends on the scalp (right side)	**Need to accept the assigned role play**
SL11	Left roleplay acceptance chakra	Tiara point where the hair band or tiara ends on the scalp (left side)	**Need to accept one's own roleplay**
SR12	Right positivity chakra	Nape of the neck (right side)	**Anticipation of adversities**
SL13	Left positivity chakra	Nape of the neck (left side)	**Anticipation of doing something wrong**

(IV) Chest Minor Chakras

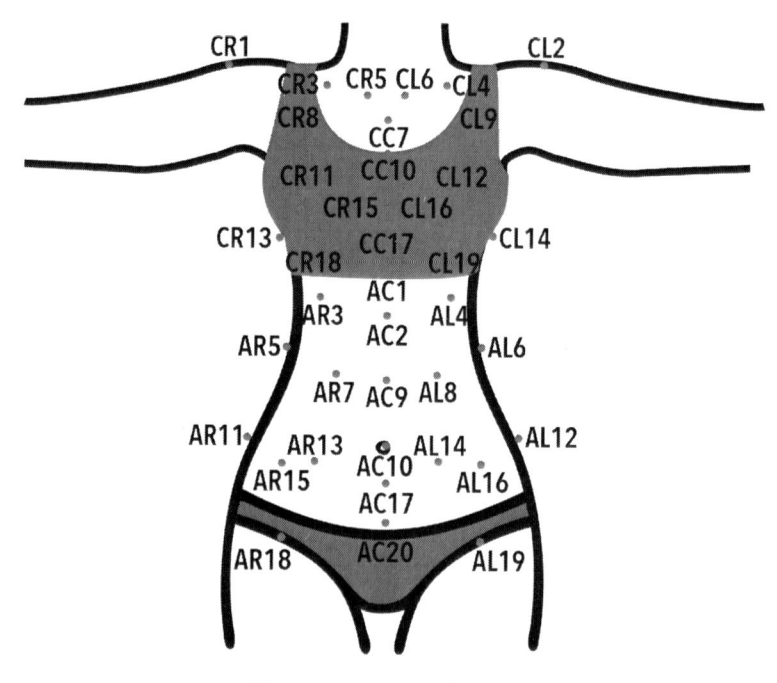

Chest & Torso Chakras

Chest Chakras

Chakra Code	Chakra Name	Position	Foundation Keyword
CR1	Right relief chakra	Right shoulder joint	Need for freedom from the past
CL2	Left relief chakra	Left Shoulder joint	Worries and concerns
CR3	Right fulfillment chakra	Clavicle (right side)	Unfulfilled feeling
CL4	Left fulfillment chakra	Clavicle (left side)	Need to fulfill self and others

Chakra Code	Chakra Name	Position	Foundation Keyword
CR5	Right courageous love chakra	Beginning of the clavicle (right side)	Need to courageously allow others to love
CL6	Left courageous love chakra	Beginning of the clavicle (left side)	Need to love courageously
CC7	Constructive compliance chakra	PAB (passive aggressive behavior)	Need for constructive approach towards the authority figures, masters, and God
CR8	Right courage chakra	Center between nipple and shoulder joint (right side)	Need to receive courageously
CL9	Left courage chakra	Center between nipple and shoulder joint (left side)	Need to contribute courageously
CC10	Acceptance chakra	Above the heart chakra (thymus)	Need for acceptance
CR11	Defensiveness chakra	Nipples (right side)	Need to defend #####
CL12	Kindness chakra	Nipples (left side)	Need to be kind
CR13	Right self-reliance chakra	Outer side of the chest (right side)	Need to receive with self-reliance
CL14	Left self-reliance chakra	Outer side of the chest (left side)	Need to contribute with self-reliance

Chakra Code	Chakra Name	Position	Foundation Keyword
CR15	Right honor chakra	Outer edge sternum at fourth costochondral joint (right side)	Need to be honorable
CL16	Left honor chakra	Outer edge sternum at fourth costochondral joint (left side)	Need to honor myself and others
CC17	Free flow chakra	Between pit of stomach and center of heart chakra	Need for the free flow
CR18	Right transparency chakra	In the crease below the nipple (right side)	Need to invite transparency and integrity from others
CL19	Left transparency chakra	In the crease below the nipple (left side)	Need to remain transparent and/or in integrity

(V) Abdomen Minor Chakras

Chakra Code	Chakra Name	Position	Foundation Keyword
AC1	Security chakra	Pit of the stomach below the sternum	Insecurity of #####
AC2	Orderliness chakra	Between solar plexus chakra and pit of stomach	The insistence of order and system
AR3	Power limitation chakra	Liver (lower rib cage - right side)	Unawareness of the power limitations

Chakra Code	Chakra Name	Position	Foundation Keyword
AL4	Potential enhancement chakra	Spleen (lower rib cage - left side)	Need to explore the potential
AR5	Right uniqueness chakra	Waist (right side)	Need to invite comparison and jealousy
AL6	Left uniqueness chakra	Waist (left side)	Need to compare and feel jealous
AR7	Structure and rule compliance chakra	Ascending colon (below liver on right side)	Difficulty in compliance with rigid rules and regulations
AL8	Structured presentation chakra	Descending colon (below spleen on left side)	Difficulty in presenting in a structured manner
AC9	Self-help chakra	Between solar plexus and navel	Helplessness
AC10	Exploration chakra	Navel	Reluctance to know the unknown Fear of the unknown
AR11	Right authority chakra	Iliac crest (right side)	Discomfort with others' demonstration of authority
AL12	Left authority chakra	Iliac crest (left side)	Discomfort with the portrayal of authority over others

Chakra Code	Chakra Name	Position	Foundation Keyword
AR13	Right compassion chakra	Iliac fossa (right side)	Feeling of being troubled, tortured, and harassed
AL14	Left compassion chakra	Iliac fossa (left side)	Feeling of torturing, troubling, harassing, or bothering self or others
AR15	Right mercy chakra	Iliac crest tip (right side)	A feeling of being revenged
AL16	Left mercy chakra	Iliac crest tip (left side)	Need to take revenge and reciprocate to others' behavior
AC17	Letting go chakra	One and half finger below navel	Inability to let go and let flow
AR18	Right synchronicity chakra	Ovary chakra (right side)	Incorrect sense of timing in receiving
AL19	Left synchronicity chakra	Ovary chakra (left side)	Incorrect sense of timing in delivering or contributing
AC20	Devotion chakra	Fold of the lower abdomen ('c' section point)	Overt sense of responsibility

(VI) Hands and Arms Minor Chakras

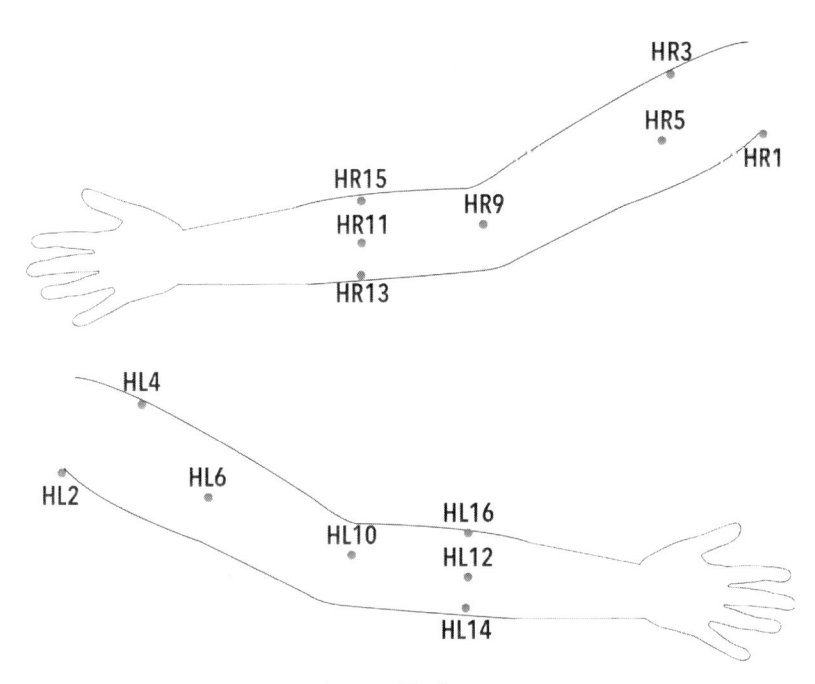

Arms Chakras

Chakra Code	Chakra Name	Position	Foundation Keyword
HR1	Right liberal approach chakra	Armpit (right)	Others' possessiveness
HL2	Left liberal approach chakra	Armpit (left)	One's own possessiveness
HR3	Right attention chakra	Deltoid (right)	**Need for attention**
HL4	Left attention chakra	Deltoid (left)	**Need to give attention**
HR5	Right harmony chakra	Bicep (right)	**Tendency to receive with struggle or fight**

Chakra Code	Chakra Name	Position	Foundation Keyword
HL6	Left harmony chakra	Bicep (left)	**Tendency to contribute with struggle or fight**
HR7	Right active withdrawal chakra	Tricep (right)	**Active withdrawal from receiving**
HL8	Left active withdrawal chakra	Tricep (left)	**Active withdrawal from giving**
HR9	Right vulnerability chakra	Elbow (right)	**Vulnerability**
HL10	Left vulnerability chakra	Elbow (left)	**Need to safeguard personal interests**
HR11	Right respect chakra	Forearm middle point (right)	**A feeling of being hated, disrespected or derogated**
HL12	Left respect chakra	Forearm middle point (left)	**Hatred/disrespect for #####**
HR13	Right freedom to command chakra	Inner forearm in alignment with baby finger (right)	**Perceived sense of pressure from authorities, preventing receiving what is necessary**
HL14	Left freedom to command chakra	Inner forearm in alignment with baby finger (Left)	**Perceived sense of pressure from authorities preventing effective contribution**

Chakra Code	Chakra Name	Position	Foundation Keyword
HR15	Right command chakra	Outer forearm in alignment with thumb (right)	Lack of command over receivables
HL16	Left command chakra	Outer forearm in alignment with thumb (left)	Lack of command over contribution

(VII) Palms Minor Chakras

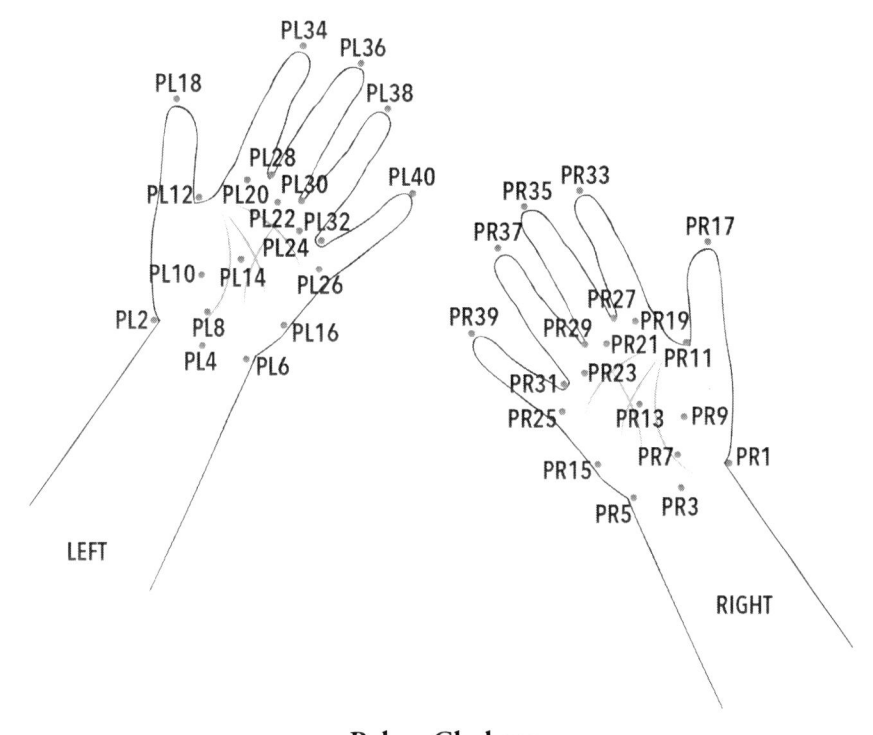

Palms Chakras

Chakra Code	Chakra Name	Position	Foundation Keyword
PR1	Right yin-yang chakra	Yin-yang point (right)	Need to fully accept the man or woman within
PL2	Left yin-yang chakra	Yin-yang point (left)	Need to accept the role play as a man or woman
PR3	Right being in the moment chakra	Wrist (right)	Need to withdraw from the past and be in the now
PL4	Left being in the moment chakra	Wrist (left)	Need to withdraw from the future and be in the now
PR5	Right polite denial chakra	Medial wrist in alignment with little finger (right)	Inability to say *no* to receiving
PL6	Left polite denial chakra	Medial wrist in alignment with little finger (left)	Inability to say *no* to contributing
PR7	Right grip chakra	Perpendicular to the wrist joint (right)	Lack of grip over the experience of receiving in life
PL8	Left grip chakra	Perpendicular to the wrist joint (left)	Inadequate grip over the contribution
PR9	Right governance chakra	Base of the thumb (right)	Having no say in the matter of receiving

Chakra Code	Chakra Name	Position	Foundation Keyword
PL10	Left governance chakra	Base of the thumb (left)	Having no say in the matter of contribution
PR11	Right dignity chakra	Groove between the thumb and index finger (right)	Need to receive with dignity
PL12	Left dignity chakra	Groove between the thumb and index finger (left)	Need contribute with dignity
PR13	Right receiving chakra	Palm (right)	Blocks in receiving
PL14	Left contribution chakra	Palm (left)	Reluctance in contribution
PR15	Right pattern break chakra	Outer edge of the palm (right)	Need to break patterns related to receiving
PL16	Left pattern break chakra	Outer edge of the palm (left)	Need to break patterns related to contribution
PR17	Right willingness chakra	Tip of the thumb (right)	Unwillingness to receive
PL18	Left willingness chakra	Tip of the thumb (left)	Unwillingness to contribute
PR19	Right career chakra	Base of the index finger (right)	Need to remain open to receive in the career or occupation

Chakra Code	Chakra Name	Position	Foundation Keyword
PL20	Left career chakra	Base of the index finger (left)	Need to appropriately contribute in the career or occupation
PR21	Right humility chakra	Base of the middle finger (right)	Need to receive with humility
PL22	Left humility chakra	Base of the middle finger (left)	Need to contribute with humility
PR23	Right beloved chakra	Base of the ring finger (right)	Feeling of being unloved
PL24	Left beloved chakra	Base of the ring finger (left)	Need to love
PR25	Right nurturance chakra	Base of the little finger (right)	Need for nurturance
PL26	Left nurturance chakra	Base of the little finger (left)	Need to nurture ######
PR27	Right deaddiction chakra	Groove between the index finger and the middle finger (right)	Addiction to or habit of receiving certain inputs and experiences
PL28	Left deaddiction chakra	Groove between the index finger and the middle finger (left)	Addiction to or habit of doing certain things
PR29	Right easy growth chakra	Groove between the middle finger and the ring finger (right)	Association of adversities in receiving with growth

Chakra Code	Chakra Name	Position	Foundation Keyword
PL30	Left easy growth chakra	Groove between the middle finger and the ring finger (left)	Association of adversities in contribution with personal or spiritual growth
PR31	Right integration chakra	Groove between the ring finger and the little finger (right)	Shattering experience of the past preventing from receiving
PL32	Left integration chakra	Groove between the ring finger and the little finger (left)	Shattering experience from the past preventing from effective contribution
PR33	Right initiative chakra	Tip of index finger (right)	Need to take initiative to receive
PL34	Left initiative chakra	Tip of index finger (left)	Need to take initiative to contribute
PR35	Right balance chakra	Tip of middle finger (right)	Need for balance in receiving
PL36	Left balance chakra	Tip of middle finger (left)	Need for balance in contribution
PR37	Right relationship chakra	Tip of ring finger (right)	Inhibitions in receiving from others in relationships

Chakra Code	Chakra Name	Position	Foundation Keyword
PL38	Left relationship chakra	Tip of ring finger (left)	Inhibitions in contributing to others in relationships
PR39	Right robustness chakra	Tip of little finger (right)	Belief of being fragile, preventing from receiving #####
PL40	Left robustness chakra	Tip of little finger (left)	Belief of being fragile preventing the effective contribution

(VIII) Back Chakras

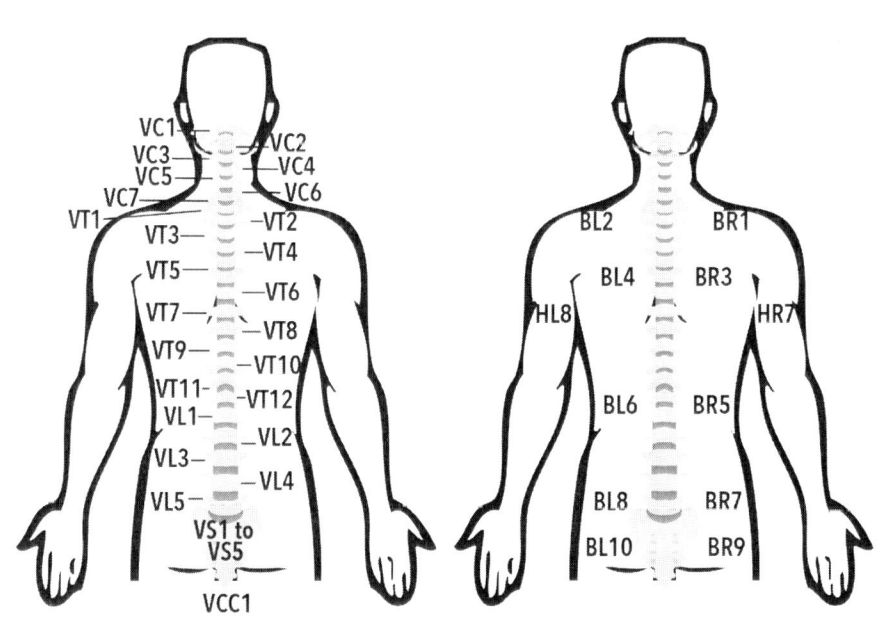

Vertebral Column Chakras

Back Chakras

Chakra Code	Chakra Name	Position	Foundation Keyword
BR1	Right smart detour chakra	Three fingers below the mid-shoulders, close to scapula	Tendency to feel blocked or sabotaged by others
BL2	Left smart detour chakra	Three fingers below the mid-shoulders, close to scapula	Tendency to block or sabotage self or others
BR3	Right faithful following chakra	Two fingers to the right of T8 vertebra	Need for backstabbing
BL4	Left faithful following chakra	Two fingers to the left of T8 vertebra	Tendency to backstab self or others

Chakra Code	Chakra Name	Position	Foundation Keyword
BR5	Right innocence chakra	Right kidney, back lumbar region	**Guilt related to parents or parent figures**
BL6	Left innocence chakra	Left kidney, back lumbar region	**Guilt related to the child or child figure**
BR7	Right comfort cruise chakra	Dimple at the level of left sacroiliac joint	**Need for tightrope walk due to external circumstances or pressures**
BL8	Left comfort cruise chakra	Dimple at the level of left sacroiliac joint	**Need to walk a tightrope**
BR9	Right motivation to move forward chakra	Right buttock (injection point)	**Need for being pushed and prodded so that you move forward and move on**
BL10	Left motivation to move forward chakra	Left buttock (injection point)	**Need to push and prod. Need to move forward and move on**

(IX) Vertebral Column Chakras

Chakra Code	Chakra Name	Position	Foundation Keyword
VC1	Horizon expansion chakra	First cervical vertebra	Limitations and boundaries
VC2	Axis chakra	Second cervical vertebra	Reminder to expand horizon by remaining aligned to the axis
VC3	Self-recognition chakra	Third cervical vertebra	Need to recognize the true self
VC4	Equality chakra	Fourth cervical vertebra	Need to feel equal to the partner or counterpart
VC5	Learning through mirroring chakra	Fifth cervical vertebra	Need to learn through mirroring others
VC6	Scope recognition chakra	Sixth cervical vertebra	Need to explore potential to make an impact on others
VC7	Liberation through isolation chakra	Seventh cervical vertebra	Need to liberate self through isolation
VT1	Positive possibility chakra	First thoracic vertebra	Need to create the space for grace and beauty

Chakra Code	Chakra Name	Position	Foundation Keyword
VT2	Director's role play chakra	Second thoracic vertebra	Need to guide others according to the higher guidance from the universe
VT3	Vulnerability acknowledgment chakra	Third thoracic vertebra	Need to convert vulnerability into strength
VT4	Refined response chakra	Fourth thoracic vertebra	Need to respond in a refined way
VT5	Collective enrolment in fun and joy chakra	Fifth thoracic vertebra	Need to enroll others to have fun and joy collectively
VT6	Reach out to unreachable ones chakra	Sixth thoracic vertebra	Need to reach out to others
VT7	Approachability chakra	Seventh thoracic vertebra	Need to remain available and approachable
VT8	Lateral thinking chakra	Eighth thoracic vertebra	Need to think creatively and differently
VT9	Reverence chakra	Ninth thoracic vertebra	Need to treat one and all with reverence
VT10	Space creation chakra	Tenth thoracic vertebra	Need to create the space for desired experiences

Chakra Code	Chakra Name	Position	Foundation Keyword
VT11	Fragrance dissemination chakra	Eleventh thoracic vertebra	**Need to be grateful to intrusive people who are helping in opening up and reach out far and wide**
VT12	Focus on master's direction chakra	Twelfth thoracic vertebra	**Need to remain focused according to the given guidance**
VL1	Brilliance chakra	First lumbar vertebra	**Need to discover the brilliance in everything**
VL2	Right alignment for gracious receiving chakra	Second lumbar vertebra	**Need to stand up for self to receive the best**
VL3	Guardianship role play active charge of your territory chakra	Third lumbar vertebra	**The role play as a guardian of ######**
VL4	Joyous reception of change chakra	Fourth lumbar vertebra	**Need to joyously welcome all changes**
VL5	Natural transition chakra	Fifth lumbar vertebra	**Need to make a natural and smooth transition to the new phase of life**
VS1	Celebration chakra	First sacral vertebra	**Need to celebrate life with people around**

Chakra Code	Chakra Name	Position	Foundation Keyword
VS2	Milestone chakra	Second sacral vertebra	**Need to celebrate every milestone and every gain**
VS3	Value chakra	Third sacral vertebra	**Need to value**
VS4	Optimism chakra	Fourth sacral vertebra	**Optimism**
VS5	Availability chakra	Fifth sacral vertebra chakra	**Availability**
VCC1	Push to be on the move chakra	The tailbone chakra	**Reluctance to continue working**

(X) Front Legs Minor Chakras

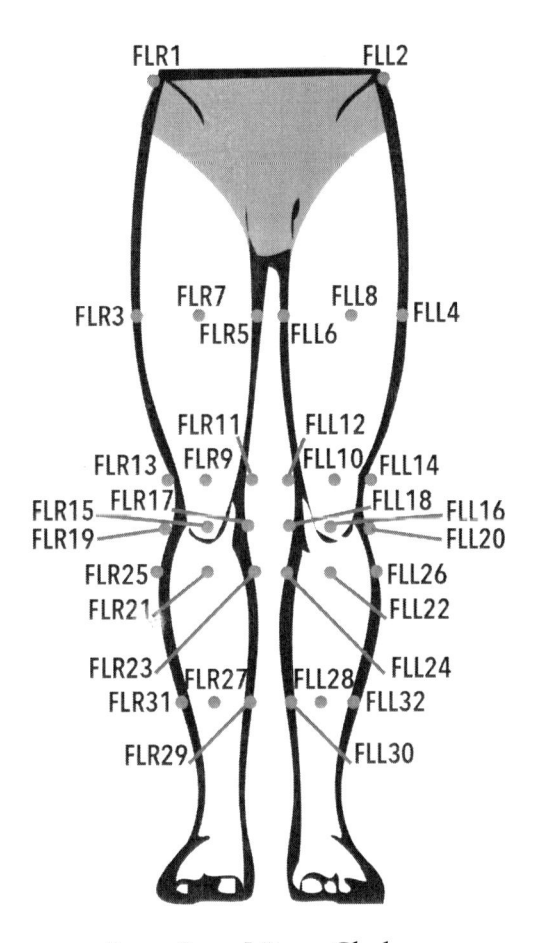

Front Legs Minor Chakras

Chakra Code	Chakra Name	Position	Foundation Keyword
FLR1	Right independence chakra	Hip joint (right)	Dependency on ##### (gadget, machine, house, etc.) from the physical material world

Chakra Code	Chakra Name	Position	Foundation Keyword
FLL2	Left independence chakra	Hip joint (left)	Dependency on ##### (name of the person one is dependent upon)
FLR3	Right detached opening up chakra	Outer thigh (right)	Reluctance to open up in a detached manner
FLL4	Left detached opening up chakra	Outer thigh (left)	Reluctance to remain open in a detached manner
FLR5	Right detached intimacy chakra	Inner thigh (right)	Reluctance to intimacy in a detached manner
FLL6	Left detached intimacy chakra	Inner thigh (left)	Reluctance to continue with intimacy in a detached manner
FLR7	Right detached security chakra	Thighs central (right)	Tendency to allow others to get attached
FLL8	Left detached security chakra	Thighs central (left)	Tendency to get attached to others
FLR9	Right humble acceptance of shortcomings chakra	Knee joint, upper part (right)	Need to mask shortcomings through ego, pride, or righteousness

Chakra Code	Chakra Name	Position	Foundation Keyword
FLL10	Left humble acceptance of shortcomings chakra	Knee joint, upper part (left)	Withdrawal due to need to the hide the shortcomings with ego, pride, and righteousness
FLR11	Right humble acceptance of shortcomings in intimacy chakra	Knee joint, upper part, inner side (right)	Ego, pride, or righteousness affecting intimate relationships
FLL12	Left humble acceptance of shortcomings in intimacy chakra	Knee joint, upper part, inner side (left)	Ego, pride, or righteousness preventing persistence in intimacy
FLR13	Right humble opening up chakra	Knee joint, upper part, outer side (right)	Need to open up keeping aside ego, pride, or righteousness
FLL14	Left humble opening up chakra	Knee joint, upper part, outer side (left)	Need to continue remaining open keeping aside ego, pride, or righteousness
FLR15	Right flexibility chakra	Knee joint, center (right)	Rigidity and inflexibility
FLL16	Left flexibility chakra	Knee joint, center (left)	Constant rigidity and inflexibility
FLR17	Right flexibility in intimate relationships chakra	Knee joint, inner side (right)	Need for flexibility in an intimate relationship

Chakra Code	Chakra Name	Position	Foundation Keyword
FLL18	Left flexibility in intimate relationships chakra	Knee joint, inner side (left)	Need for ongoing flexibility in an intimate relationship
FLR19	Right flexibility in opening up chakra	Knee joint, outer side (right)	Need to open up with flexibility
FLL20	Left flexibility in opening up chakra	Knee joint, outer side (left)	Need to continue remaining open with flexibility
FLR21	Right surrender chakra	Knee joint, lower part (right)	Need to surrender to the higher consciousness
FLL22	Left surrender chakra	Knee joint, lower part (left)	Need to continue surrendering to the higher consciousness
FLR 23	Right intimacy with surrender chakra	Knee joint, lower part, inner side (right)	Reluctance to surrender to the higher consciousness for the welfare of intimate relationships
FLL24	Left intimacy with surrender chakra	Knee joint, lower part, inner side (left)	Reluctance to continue surrendering to the higher consciousness for the welfare of intimate relationships

Chakra Code	Chakra Name	Position	Foundation Keyword
FLR25	Right opening up with surrender chakra	Knee joint, lower part, outer side (right)	Difficulty in opening up by surrendering
FLL26	Left opening up with surrender chakra	Knee joint, lower part, outer side (left)	Difficulty in remaining open by surrendering
FLR27	Right cushioning chakra	Shin bone, front part of the leg (right)	Need for cushioning and buffering
FLL28	Left cushioning chakra	Shin bone, front part of the leg (left)	Need for constant cushioning and buffering
FLR29	Right hurt-free intimacy chakra	Inner side of lower legs (right)	Difficulty in intimacy due to stored emotional hurt
FLL30	Left hurt-free intimacy chakra	Inner side of lower legs (left)	Need to withdraw from intimate relationships due to stored emotional hurts
FLR31	Right hurt-free opening up chakra	Outer side of lower legs (right)	Stored emotional hurts preventing from opening up
FLL32	Left hurt-free opening up chakra	Outer side of lower legs (left)	Stored emotional hurts preventing from remaining open

(XI) Back Legs Minor Chakras

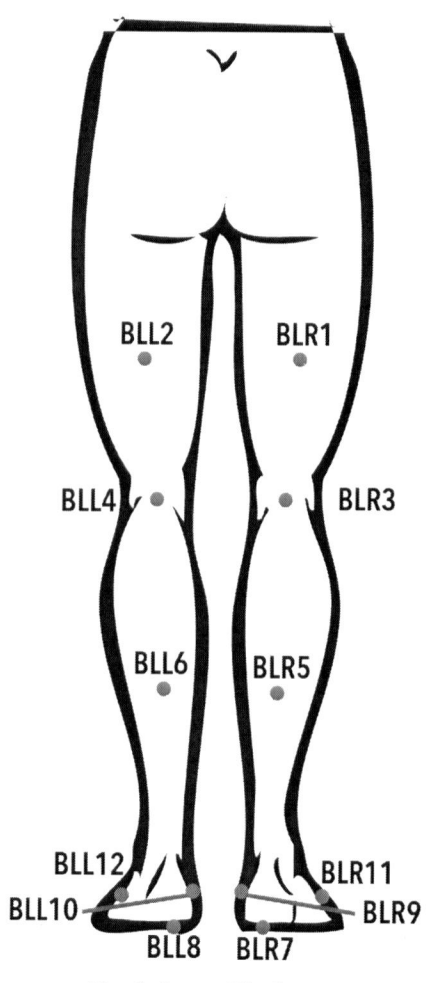

Back Legs Chakras

Chakra Code	Chakra Name	Position	Foundation Keyword
BLR1	Right detachment chakra	Back thigh, center point (right)	**Indifference from others**
BLL2	Left detachment chakra	Back thigh, center point (left)	**Indifference**

Chakra Code	Chakra Name	Position	Foundation Keyword
BLR3	Right constancy chakra	Back of knee joint (right)	Aversion to constancy
BLL4	Left constancy chakra	Back of knee joint (left)	Constant need for change
BLR5	Right emotional hurt release chakra	Calf muscle (right)	Stored emotional hurts
BLL6	Left emotional hurt release chakra	Calf muscle (left)	Need to withdraw due to stored emotional hurts
BLR7	Right fair redistribution of the brunt chakra	Heel (right)	Tendency to invite, inherit or borrow problems
BLL8	Left fair redistribution of the brunt chakra	Heel (left)	Constant tendency to invite, inherit or borrow problems
BLR9	Right intimacy with fair redistribution of the brunt chakra	Inner heel (right)	Association of intimate relationships with troubles and problems
BLL10	Left intimacy with fair redistribution of the brunt chakra	Inner heel (left)	Constant association of intimate relationships with troubles and problems

Chakra Code	Chakra Name	Position	Foundation Keyword
BLR11	Right opening up with fair redistribution of the brunt chakra	Outer heel (right)	**Reluctance to open up due to the possibility of inviting troubles or suffering**
BLL12	Left opening up with fair redistribution of brunt chakra	Outer heel (left)	**Reluctance to remain open due to the possibility of inviting troubles or suffering**

(XII) Toes and Feet Minor Chakras

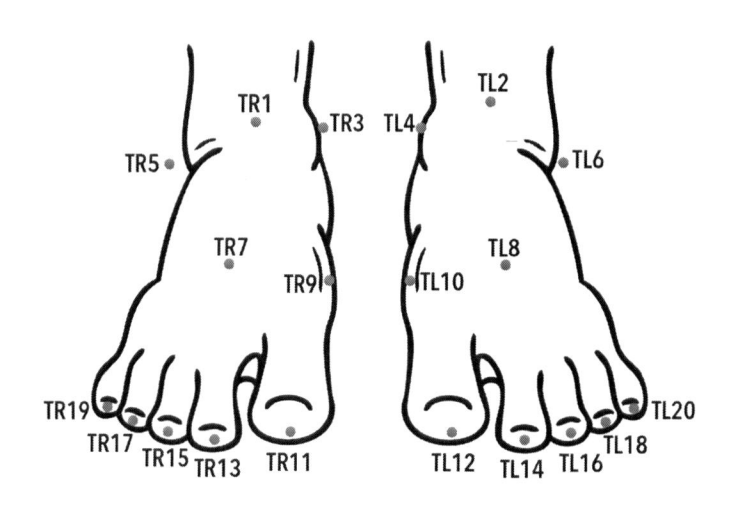

Feet Chakras

Chakra code	Chakra name	Position	Foundation keyword
TR1	Right strength chakra	Ankle (right)	A sense of shortcoming or weakness
TL2	Left strength chakra	Ankle (left)	Need to withdraw due to constant feeling of shortcomings or weakness
TR3	Right intimacy with inner strength chakra	Inner ankle (right)	Association of intimate relationships with weakness
TL4	Left intimacy with inner strength chakra	Inner ankle (left)	Ongoing association of intimate relationship with weakness
TR5	Right opening up with inner strength chakra	Outer ankle (right)	Association of opening up with weakness or shortcomings
TL6	Left opening up with inner strength chakra	Outer ankle (left)	Ongoing association of opening up with weakness or shortcomings
TR7	Right win-win option chakra	Dorsal of the foot (right)	Feeling of being exploited due to the need to be needed

Chakra code	Chakra name	Position	Foundation keyword
TL8	Left win-win option chakra	Dorsal of the foot (left)	Ongoing feeling of being exploited due to the need to be needed
TR9	Right ground reality acceptance chakra	Arch of the foot (right)	Inability to come to terms with the ground reality
TL10	Left ground reality acceptance chakra	Arch of the foot (left)	Reluctance to come to terms with ground reality
TR11	Right best foot forward chakra	Great toe (right)	Reluctance to put the best foot forward
TL12	Left best foot forward chakra	Great toe (left)	Resistance to continue putting the best foot forward
TR13	Right cooperation chakra	Second toe (right)	Need to attract domination, competition, and non-cooperation
TL14	Left cooperation chakra	Second toe (left)	Need to withdraw due to perceived possibility of domination, competition, and one-upmanship

Chakra code	Chakra name	Position	Foundation keyword
TR15	Right contribution in relationships chakra	Third toe (right)	Need to contribute in relationships
TL16	Left contribution in relationships chakra	Third toe (left)	Need to continue contributing in relationships
TR17	Right artistic expression of love chakra	Fourth toe (right)	Need to express love in a creative way
TL18	Left artistic expression of love chakra	Fourth toe (left)	Need to continue expressing love in a creative way
TR19	Right focus chakra	Little toe (right)	Need to be focused
TL20	Left focus chakra	Little toe (left)	Need for being consistently focused

The Redikall Crystalline Mind is a foundation course and a major stepping stone in the Redikall Insights Curriculum. It can also be a stand-alone self-management and self-healing technique. The guidebook can give you knowledge and insights. However, you can experience a profound shift when you learn under supervision and guidance from qualified and experienced expert.

Redikall Insights curriculum makes it very easy for you to identify, modify, and amplify a "radical" thought to bring in a radical transformative shift in your life.

Redikall Curriculum is for those individuals who opt for a systematic evolution through inner resolution and outer revolution

Appendix II: About Redikall Insights

Redikall Insights is the art of enjoying a super life with Superconscious Mind. Redikall Insights offers you an integrated curriculum of various techniques and self-management tools you can use to recognize, modify, and amplify your precise thoughts, which can inspire a positive shift in your life.

The Story of Redikall

Way back in 2006, Aatmn, a senior homeopathic physician and a seeker of life, in her deep meditative state, got in touch with the intuitive knowledge of five minor chakras. As she sought further guidance on the purpose and use of knowledge of these five minor chakras, she was directed exactly to the process of designing statements based on these chakras' knowledge.

The same evening, some of her students approached her with minor complaints such as a common cold and pain caused by knee joint problems. She used the intuitive knowledge of those five minor chakras, and they created an instant shift within her students. They started feeling better immediately.

She was astonished with the results and was totally convinced about the value of the intuitive knowledge. She started keeping a pen and a diary handy so she could note down most of the information she got in her meditative space.

When she reached her office after a week, she shared this amazing healing work with some of her students there. As they kept asking questions, she continued checking various minor chakras and further intuitive answers while replying to all requesting her for solutions. She clinically verified them on several students and patients. Some of her students took diligent notes and presented her with a document they called Redikall Healing Notes and requested her to conduct a workshop.

Over a period of time, Aatmn fine-tuned this workshop and taught diverse people spread out over India and abroad, including individuals, groups from schools, corporations, and NGOs. She employed online as well as classroom workshop modes.

Aatmn freely shares this knowledge and keeps in touch with her students from all over the world.

Later, Redikall Healing obtained the legal copyright so that the knowledge can be spread through the right channels in a correct way.

Redikall Crystalline Mind, which is the foundation course to the Redikall Insights curriculum, has been designed, by request, by one of her students with an objective to study the effects of the Redikall Insights curriculum on a group of women. This was a project study for her post-graduate work in psychology.

What is Redikall Healing?

Redikall Healing is the intuitive art of healing at a radical level. It is also an integral essence of Redikall Insights Curriculum. Redikall Healing is facilitated by recognizing and modifying your causative thoughts and amplifying your curative thoughts. The ultimate objective of Redikall Healing System is to assist an individual to connect to the higher consciousness facilitating the possibility of leading a fulfilled, harmonious and balanced life guided by their ultimate consciousness.

Redikall Insights is a self-management curriculum taught through workshops, webinars, and mentorship programs. It prepares you to manage yourself and guide others to manage themselves in a radically different way with an objective to lead life with a consistent experience of joy, peace, fulfillment, and completion. Most of the challenges, issues, and problems are resolved as a byproduct when Redikall practitioners align their thinking with their highest consciousness.

The root cause of every "dis-ease" is a thought. Redikall Facilitation involves diagnosing this thought, reversing it with the appropriate Redikall Statement, and reconfirming the new thought. If the Redikall Statement is appropriate, the chakras will be resonantly open and will provide an immediate shift or pain relief. Also, a perceivable shift in the "being" is often accompanied by a sigh of relief as the light of a positive thought induced by a correctly designed Redikall statement dispels the energy congestion caused by the erroneous thought process. Of course, at times, the environment and the resultant response to the environment does affect our thoughts. However, correcting the thought brings in refined responses which eventually shift the physical reality in a constructive manner.

We have observed that there are two types of problems and challenges: Only 20 percent of the challenges are strategically interwoven in life with a brilliant purpose and divine plan. The remaining 80 percent of challenges are caused by our adverse response based on the ignorance of the brilliance behind the challenges. We can address this 80 percent by refining our responses while the remaining 20 percent of challenges can be better addressed if we discover and align to the purpose and brilliance offered by them.

In a nutshell, the Redikall Insights Curriculum helps you in the following ways:

1. Recognizing and reorganizing your thoughts
2. Refining your responses
3. Experiencing relief from physical and emotional pain
4. Inference of subtle communication through the perception of various adversities
5. Finding answers, solutions, and directions
6. Better understanding self and others
7. Enhanced problem-solving capacity

8. Consulting skills to assist and guide others in their decision making and problem solving
9. Personal and spiritual growth
10. A superconscious life with total awareness of who you are and why things are the way they are

We do not claim it to be an alternative healing system. Correction in the thought process, assisted by the Redikall Insights, can facilitate the healing process. Redikall Healing can complement any prevalent healing or therapeutic system, or it can be a wonderful self-management life transformation system for a preventive and proactive approach towards individual health and life in general.

Redikall Today

Today, Redikall Insights is facilitated and taught by workshop facilitators who are trained and certified personally by Aatmn on behalf of Omnipresence Academy of Life Pvt. Ltd. She occasionally teaches special groups, and also teaches through the internet via various online channels. Her mission is to inspire people to remain acutely aware of their personal powers of the 'thought manifestation' so that they could use their powerful asset appropriately and bring about the positive transformation in their life and others' life around them. Her vision is to ensure interconnectivity between the physical and metaphysical world to restore harmony amongst individuals and amongst all elements.

Now, with her in-depth knowledge and enhanced awareness, she has designed the Redikall Insights Curriculum, which includes the courses outlined in the following table:

Level	Course Name	Mode of Learning	Eligibility
1	**Redikall Crystalline Mind**	Book, webinar, workshops	Open to all

2	**Essential Redikall Insights Course**	Workshops and webinars	Omnipresence Academy of Life–certified participants of Redikall Crystalline Mind workshop
3	**Advanced Redikall Consciousness Course**	Workshops and retreats	Omnipresence Academy of Life–certified participants of Essential Redikall Insights Course
4	**Redikall Relationships**	Four-day retreat	Omnipresence Academy of Life–certified participants of Advanced Redikall Healing Course
5	**Redikall Money and Maya**	Five-day retreat	By invitation
6	**The Redikall Retreat**	Seven-day retreat	By invitation

Redikall note: The curriculum is periodically upgraded and changed. For the latest curriculum, and other online courses/workshops/mentorship program, please visit www.redikallhealing.com

Appendix III: Redikall Reorganization Statements

First set of Redikall Reorganization Statements

- I revive this *****
- I recognize this *****
- I realign this *****
- I reorient this *****
- I reposition this *****
- I revive the reason behind this *****
- I recognize the reason behind this *****
- I realign the reason behind this *****
- I reorient the reason behind this *****
- I reposition the reason behind this *****
- I revive the brilliance in this *****
- I recognize the brilliance in this *****
- I realign the brilliance in this *****
- I reorient the brilliance in this *****
- I reposition the brilliance in this *****

Second set of Redikall Reorganization Statements (for resistance)

- I revive my resistance to be free from this *****
- I recognize my resistance to be free from this *****
- I realign my resistance to be free from this *****
- I reorient my resistance to be free from this *****
- I reposition my resistance to be free from this *****
- I revive the reason behind my resistance to be free from this *****
- I recognize the reason behind my resistance to be free from this *****

- I realign the reason behind my resistance to be free from this *****
- I reorient the reason behind my resistance to be free from this *****
- I reposition the reason behind my resistance to be free from this *****
- I revive the brilliance in my resistance to be free from this *****
- I recognize the brilliance in my resistance to be free from this *****
- I realign the brilliance in my resistance to be free from this *****
- I reorient the brilliance in my resistance to be free from this *****
- I reposition the brilliance in my resistance to be free from this *****

Appendix IV: Redikall FAQs

Q: What are Chakras?

A: Chakras are powerful energy centers in your energy body (aura). Your adverse thoughts have a tendency to block them and interfere with the energy flow. Each chakra has a tendency to attract a particular theme of thoughts. Blocked energy flow indicates the need to correct a particular set of beliefs or thoughts. You have seven major chakras as traditionally described and several minor chakras as described in Redikall by Aatmn.

Q: What is the difference between Crystalline Mind, Redikall Foundation Technique, and Redikall Reorganization Statements?

A: The achievement of a Crystalline Mind is the end objective of using the Redikall Foundation Technique. Redikall Reorganization statements are integral part of the Redikall Foundation Technique.

Q: What is the difference between Redikall Statements, affirmations and positive affirmations?

A: Redikall Statements are affirmations that are designed in alignment with Redikall Philosophy, based on minor chakra knowledge, knowledge of the subconscious mind, metaphysics, and channelled information from higher consciousness compiled as the Redikall Curriculum. These are not the same as positive affirmations. They often employ words considered negative by some that are meant to bring these so-called negative thoughts to our awareness for the purpose of reorganization in an appropriate way.

Q: Isn't it dangerous to affirm negative words?

A: These statements work on the principle 'similia similibus curantur' This statement was described by Dr. Hahnemann, the founder of the homeopathic system of medicine, and it is mentioned in Sanskrit and Greek literature too. It means that a poison can take care of poison, somewhat like a vaccine (antidote effect). When we ignore our painful experiences, they go unattended or at times worsen. The "negative" words that are occasionally used in some of the Redikall Reorganization statements often trigger our dormant thoughts and emotions so that our conscious minds can reorganize and restore them in the most appropriate way.

Q: What is the conscious mind?

A: The conscious mind is the part of the mind to which we are normally present. This part of the mind thinks in a linear fashion, considers logics, calculates data, and takes logical decisions.

Q: What is the subconscious mind?

A: The subconscious mind is the part of the mind we are not regularly in touch with. This part of the mind stores information. It is preprogrammed to keep us alive, and it thinks in an abstract way while it remains influenced by and connected to the metaphysical realm.

Q: What is the superconscious mind?

A: From the Redikall perspective, the superconscious mind is a Crystalline Mind which remains well connected to the Prime Resource Energy for the guidance, direction and effective functioning. It serves as a bridge between the physical and metaphysical realms, and its purpose is to enrich life in the physical realm with greater consciousness. The ultimate objective of the Redikall Insights Curriculum is to facilitate your evolution from Conscious Mind to Superconscious Mind.

Q: What is the higher consciousness? A: The higher consciousness is the part of our "being" that can observe and guide us from an evolved perspective. We can establish a conscious connection with the higher consciousness when the filter mind is cleared and the subconscious mind is fairly reorganized.

Q: What is meditation?

A: Meditation is a way of life in which one experiences a total alignment between the Prime Resource Energy, higher consciousness, metaphysical world, physical world, the conscious mind, and the subconscious mind. Meditation can clear the filter mind and facilitate the reorganization of the storage system in your subconscious mind. While there are several techniques to meditate, essentially meditation is a way of life. With regular practice, you can live in a state of bliss and experience joy, peace, greater clarity, and a refined response system—all of which helps you to lead life in a meaningful manner. There are several techniques that can be used to achieve this state. The Redikall Foundation Technique and several other techniques are taught in the Redikall curriculum, can assist you in remaining in this state with greater awareness.

Q: How long does the positive effect of the shift last?

A: A lot depends upon the issue being addressed. If the issue is closer to the core, the effect is long lasting.

Q: Will the issue recur?

A: If you have done in-depth work and addressed the core, generated inner awareness of the reasons behind the issue, the chances of recurrence are minimum. However, the issues of life are reminders for deeper-level correction. Issues can recur mildly and occasionally to remind you and make you aware. They can also recur if you have not addressed your association of the problem with growth. Some of the challenges are brilliantly designed as an integral part of the life plan, like pillars in a monument. At times, you may have to recognize and align yourself with the brilliance offered by them. Fortunately, they are very few.

Q: I am using Redikall Reorganization statements, but they are not working.

A: Please make sure you are designing your Redikall Reorganization statements (RRS) on the following guidelines:

- For physical discomfort, you are designing the RRS based on associated emotions or resultant feelings.
- You are correctly applying and using metaphor. For example, if a person is feeling sad and if he describes sadness "as if a log of wood is kept over my chest", the person should design his Redikall Reorganization statements with the words *a log of wood* instead of working directly with sadness. For example, "I revive the log of wood, I reposition the log of wood …" (Refer to Appendix III.)
- You may want to address the advantage of continuing to be in the problem; for example, sympathy or avoidance of work.
- You may address the fear of being problem free.
- You can also address any resistance you may feel.
- You may also address any inhibitory beliefs you may have.
- If there are structural changes in the body, such as advanced osteoarthritis, tumors, cancer, or bone fractures, the reversal may or may not happen, but you can shift your approach and gain emotional neutrality to manage your body's ailments.
- You may consult a Redikall Facilitator or mentor online or in your town to seek further guidance.

Please note: The 'Redikall' is not an alternative healing system. This is a mind management and awareness enhancement system, which naturally complements any therapeutic work. Additionally, it generates awareness by decoding the subtle communication offered by your body's ailments or seeming adversities in your life.

Contact Us

Omnipresence Academy of Life Pvt. Ltd.

Phone: +91-80808-09371

Website: www.redikallhealing.com